Joseph Parrish Thompson

Love and Penalty

Eternal punishment consistent with the fatherhood of God

Joseph Parrish Thompson

Love and Penalty
Eternal punishment consistent with the fatherhood of God

ISBN/EAN: 9783337368449

Printed in Europe, USA, Canada, Australia, Japan

Cover: Foto ©Lupo / pixelio.de

More available books at **www.hansebooks.com**

LOVE AND PENALTY;

OR,

ETERNAL PUNISHMENT

CONSISTENT WITH THE

FATHERHOOD OF GOD.

BY JOSEPH P. THOMPSON, D.D.,

PASTOR OF THE BROADWAY TABERNACLE CHURCH.

New-York:
SHELDON & COMPANY, 115 Nassau Street.
BOSTON . GOULD & LINCOLN.
1860.

TO THE

MEMORY

OF

NATHANIEL W. TAYLOR, D.D.,

WHO FIRST TAUGHT ME

"TO JUSTIFY THE WAYS OF GOD TO MEN,"

This volume is inscribed with grateful and reverent affection

In preparing the following Lectures for the press, I have retained the form of direct personal address in which they were delivered to a popular assembly, but have expanded some points of verbal criticism to an extent not admissible in mere pulpit discourse. I trust that without sacrificing the popular character of the discussion, I have made it more acceptable to the scholarly reader. The sixth and ninth lectures have been added to the original series.

NEW YORK, *Sept.* 1860.   J. P. T.

NEW YORK, *November* 7, 1859.

REV. J. P. THOMPSON, D.D.:

Dear Sir—We cannot withhold the expression of our appreciation of the Series of Sabbath Evening Discourses delivered by you, on *The Future Punishment of the Wicked, as consistent with the Paternal Character of God*.

The sophistical views recently advanced through some of our popular monthlies, as well as by certain "leading" men; the prevailing tendency of the age to the adoption of new ideas, without *thorough* inquiry; and the welcome extended to every thought that might serve to quiet the unregenerate heart, seem to us to have demanded this examination.

We rejoice that you have so faithfully and eloquently performed this service.

Believing that there is not accessible to the reading public so complete a refutation of these errors, we, for the many Christians with whom we are daily brought in contact, as well as for ourselves, beg you will be induced to place the entire series in the hands of your publisher, that all who would "rest on the promises" may have at hand this " word in season " as a help and guide, and that the warnings to those in danger, which you have so plainly and kindly uttered, may reach a still larger number.

With warm assurances of our regard and esteem, we are.

Very truly, yours,

HENRY WHITTELSEY,	MYRON H. CLARK,
THOMAS RITTER,	F. F. THOMPSON,
JAMES SMITH,	S. W. BENEDICT,
MATTHEW W. STARR, Jr.,	ABSALOM PETERS,
WM. G. WEST,	MILTON BADGER,
A. K. THOMPSON,	A. A. FISHER,
H. F. BEEBE,	DAVID N. BEEBE,
WILLIAM B. HOLMES,	J. E. FISHER,
W. E. CALDWELL,	ALEX. ANDERSON,
JAMES D. SMITH,	ADON SMITH,
THOS. E. SMITH,	R. O. MASON,
SAMUEL HOLMES,	L. RANNEY,
AUSTIN ABBOTT,	FRAS. B. NICOL,
OLIVER BARRATT,	L. M. BATES,
HENRY HAYES,	S. BARTLETT, Jr.,
JNO. C. TAYLOR,	IRA O. MILLER,
H. UNDERWOOD,	N. A. CALKINS,
J. GAMALIEL RILEY.	THOMAS LANE,
E. L. CHAMPLIN,	C. H. WATERBURY,
WM. W. FESSENDEN,	SAMUEL P. HOLMES,
ROE LOCKWOOD,	EDWARD PRATT,

HENRY C. HALL.

MESSRS. H. WHITTELSEY AND OTHERS:

My Dear Friends—I thank you for the favorable terms in which you are pleased to express yourselves with regard to my recent course of lectures on Future Retribution. I was led to prepare those discourses by a deep conviction of the need of a thorough, and at the same time popular, discussion of the doctrine of Eternal Punishment, at once to invigorate the faith of Christians and to counteract the influence of the modern schools of Rationalistic Infidelity. I am thankful that this effort has received your approbation, and this encourages me to commit the Lectures to the press, in the hope of a wider and more permanent usefulness. With high respect, &c.,

Yours, in the bonds of the Gospel

JOSEPH P. THOMPSON.

NEW YORK, *November* 9, 1859

CONTENTS.

LECTURE		PAGE
I.	Divine Retribution Argued from the Constitution of the Human Mind	7
II.	Future Retribution Argued from the Course of Providence in this World	62
III.	Future Retribution Argued from the Fatherhood of God in Christ	93
IV.	Future Retribution Argued from the Demerit of Sin	125
V.	No Future Probation Revealed or Probable	161
VI.	The Immortality of the Soul	198
VII.	Eternal Punishment a Doctrine of the Bible	265
VIII.	Punishment, not Annihilation, the Future Portion of the Ungodly	295
IX.	The Paternal Character of God a Pledge that he will Punish Sin	333

LECTURE I.

DIVINE RETRIBUTION ARGUED FROM THE CONSTITUTION OF THE HUMAN MIND.

John iii: 35, 36. *The Father loveth the Son, and hath given all things into his hand. He that believeth on the Son hath everlasting life; and he that believeth not the Son shall not see life; but the wrath of God abideth on him.*

A PREACHER of some notoriety, who boasted that his reason had emancipated him from the "Ecclesiastical Theology of Christendom," has given this account of the process of that emancipation. "In my early childhood, after a severe but silent struggle, I made way with the ghastly doctrine of Eternal Damnation and a Wrathful God; this is the Goliath of that Theology. From my seventh year I have had no *Fear* of God, only an ever-greatening Love and Trust."*

Jesus Christ said "*Fear* Him who is able to destroy both soul and body in hell." And did not Christ know God, and love and trust Him as the infinite Father?

Mr. Parker further tells us that the "ecclesiastical theology" attributes to God "an imperfect and cruel character." But that humble and sincere preacher, John the Baptist, in the text exhibits God as a Father delighting in Christ his Son, and yet as capable of wrath. And Jesus, in the very sermon on the mount in which he portrays the love of God as a Father, warns men lest through an excessive love of this world they should be cast into hell.† Either then Mr. Parker quite misapprehends the character of God, or Christ and the preachers of the New Testament misapprehended or misrepresented his character. Another preacher, also

---

* "Theodore Parker's Experience as a Minister," p. 35.

† Matt. 5 : 27—31.

of celebrity in the circles of literature and philanthropy, in a lately published sermon, says, " When Jesus out of the fullness of an immeasurable trust, calls God Father, we are sure that God *is* Father. That heart definition is the right definition." . . And then he asks " whether a *woman's* heart would ever have admitted into its theology a devil and an angry God, or have conceived of accursed humanity or an everlasting hell."* But the apostle John, the disciple whom Jesus loved, and to whom he commended his own mother, whose heart was tender and loving as a woman's, who teaches us that God is love, and makes love the test of fellowship with God,—this most gentle and amiable of disciples declares that " he that committeth sin is of the devil," and that " whoso is not written in the book of life shall be cast into the lake of fire." And Jesus, when he introduces God as the Father, in that high and solemn scene " when the Son of man shall come in his glory," represents himself as

* Rev. O. B. Frothingham.

saying to those upon his right hand, "Come ye blessed of my Father," and to those on the left hand, "Depart from me ye cursed, into everlasting fire prepared for the devil and his angels."* These words " devil," " hell " and " fire," are not the invention of what one of these modern preachers calls the " ecclesiastical theology," and the other, the " cold French intellect of hard-headed," " chilly," " unimaginative and lawless John Calvin." These words were freely used by the lovely and loving John the Apostle, who himself had learned them from the lips of that Jesus who has taught us to call God, Father.

There is a mistake then somewhere; our modern preacher fails to apprehend the whole character of God, fails especially to apprehend the consistency of love with retributive justice, or John and Jesus did not understand the character of the Father whom they preached.

A prominent philanthropist, of great purity of character and gentleness of spirit, has

---

* Matt. 25 : 34 and 41.

lately published to the world his "Religion of Reason," in which he asks:

"Would Jesus have told us to set no limits to the times of forgiving our brother, had he believed that the exercise of God's forgiving spirit is confined to this brief stage of human existence? Would he have told us to be so much better than he believed God to be?"[*] But Jesus *did* say, "He that shall blaspheme against the Holy Ghost, hath *never* forgiveness, but is in danger of eternal damnation. Either Jesus misrepresents God, or our philanthropist does not understand his character.

Our philanthropist exclaims, " Putting people into an eternal hell! why, the worst of men would not thus serve their worst enemies. How much less would God! Orthodoxy makes God infinitely more malignant and cruel than are the most malignant and cruel men." But Jesus, who was the only perfect philanthropist the world has ever seen, declares that when he shall come in the judg-

---

[*] Three Discourses on the "Religion of Reason," by Gerrit Smith, p. 50.

ment, he will himself consign to an eternal hell those who have not lived in this world according to his Gospel. Jesus, the Savior of men, Jesus " who went about doing good," Jesus who " came to seek and save the lost," Jesus, whose love for man led him to renounce all earthly honor, and to accept poverty, reproach, suffering, and death, tells us that He himself will say to those upon his left hand, " Depart from me into everlasting fire;—and these shall go away into everlasting punishment."* Either then our modern philanthropist is mistaken in the assertion that the doctrine of eternal punishment makes God malignant and cruel, or Jesus Christ was the most malignant and cruel of men, and the God whom he taught us to call our Father *is* a being of infinite malignity.

I accept that issue—for it is the pointblank issue of all this denial of future punishment as inconsistent with the benignity of God. If the argument of these gentlemen is sound, I, for one, cannot stop short of the log-

---

* Matt. 25 : 41 and 46.

ical honesty of the first, who admitted that the New Testament does teach eternal punishment, and therefore denied its authority over his religious belief.

A popular author, representing the "Broad Church" party in the Church of England, in a preface to a recent edition of a religious novel of the last century, satirizes the current theology of the "evangelical" school, as teaching in effect that "nothing can be known of God's character, even from the person of Jesus Christ, save that he will doom to endless torture the vast majority of the human race, while he has made, for the purpose of delivering a very small minority, a certain highly artificial arrangement, to be explained by no human notions of justice or of love."* But setting aside the gross injustice of this caricature upon those who hold the doctrines of eternal punishment and divine election, there still remain these declarations of our Lord; "Wide is the gate, and broad is the

---

* Rev. Charles Kingsley, M. A., Preface to Brooke's "Fool of Quality."

way, that leadeth to *destruction* [or perdition —the opposite of " life "], and *many* there be which go in thereat : because strait is the gate and narrow is the way, which leadeth unto life [a state of secure and blessed existence], and *few* there be that find it." There still remains this devout thanksgiving of Paul " Blessed be the God and Father of our Lord Jesus Christ. . . . . who hath chosen, us in Him before the foundation of the world, . . . having predestinated unto the adoption of children by Jesus Christ to himself, according to the good pleasure of his will." If this be a "highly artificial arrangement," the apostle records it to "the praise of the glory of the grace " of God the *Father;* whom he elsewhere represents as as having " endured with much long suffering the vessels of wrath fitted to destruction," and yet making known " the riches of his glory in the vessels of mercy which he had afore prepared unto glory, even us whom he hath *called."* Either Paul and Christ misapprehended the condition of mankind and the plan of redemption, or these declarations must somehow be explained by "human notions of justice and of love."

A profound British essayist condemns the "Christian morality" of our times as a system of "legality," which "holds out the hope of heaven and the threat of hell, as the appointed and appropriate motives to a virtuous life."* If by this statement he would convey the impression that the body of Christian theologians and teachers make future rewards and punishments the sole, or even the principal motives to a virtuous life, he misrepresents them as grievously as he charges that they misrepresent "the morality of the New Testament." But if he intends to deny that the system of morality taught by Christ and the apostles "holds out the hope of heaven and the threat of hell as *appointed and appropriate* motives to a virtuous life," we find him in controversy with these declarations of our Lord; "If thine eye offend thee [by inciting unchaste desire] pluck it out, and

---

* John Stuart Mill; Essay on Liberty, p. 89.

cast it from thee; it is *better* for thee to enter into life with one eye, rather than having two eyes to be cast into hell-fire;"—"Fear Him who hath power to cast both soul and body into hell;"—we find him in controversy with Paul's account of his motives and method in preaching—"We must all appear before the judgment seat of Christ; that every one may receive the things done in his body, according to that he hath done, whether it be good or bad. Knowing therefore the *terror* of the Lord we *persuade* men." A reverential sense of his own accountability to Christ made Paul faithful in proclaiming his gospel; and he sought to persuade men to accept Christ as well by a salutary dread of the final judgment as by the hope of salvation. Be its morality true or false, the New Testament does use the threat of hell as an appropriate motive to a virtuous life. We may not set aside its declarations by a foregone conclusion of our philosophy; but should honestly examine them in the light of reason and by the comparison of Scripture with itself.

I do not quote these opinions of others with a view to controversy, but as examples of modes of thought and argument which illustrate the gravity of the question under discussion; and I have taken the statements of writers and preachers widely known for their intelligence, integrity, and philanthropy, in order to set forth the opposition to the doctrine of Eternal Punishment with whatever weight of ability and character it can fairly claim. I adduce no weight of authority upon the other side; no catalogue of great and good men who hold this as a doctrine of the Scriptures. The appeal must lie not to names and authorities, but to the word of God and the principles of his Moral Government, as interpreted by an enlightened reason and an honest heart. For myself, I will not hold any article of faith which I cannot intelligently and honestly defend by Reason and the Scriptures.

It will be observed that the point and stress of these objections is, that the future punishment of the wicked, and especially an eternal retribution, is incompatible with the character of God as a *Father*. It is to this point, mainly, that I shall address myself in the argument of this and succeeding discourses. The text brings these two aspects of the divine character—the FATHER as revealed in Christ, and the vindicative JUDGE and PUNISHER of sin, into immediate and indissoluble connection. "The Father loveth the Son, and hath given all things into his hand; He that believeth on the Son hath everlasting life; and he that believeth not the Son shall not see life; but the wrath of God —οργη, indignation that leads to punishment —the punitive wrath of God abideth upon him." This passage exhibits what one has finely styled " the *equilibrium* of the divine character;" an equilibrium of attributes which the Scriptures always maintain; whereas " the tendency of the human mind, left to itself, is ever to a partial view—to an effeminate sentimentalism on the one hand, or to a dark fanaticism on the other—to an unwarranted trust in the Divine mercy, untempered by any regard to that justice which gives mercy all its value, or to those gloomy apprehensions of wrath, which arise from the sole contemplation of the sterner attributes of the Deity."* The Scriptures present God as a Father, and in the same breath denounce - "the wrath of God" upon those who refuse the highest expression of his love, in the gift of Christ his Son.

It will be the aim of this series of Lectures to show that *the doctrine of the Eternal Punishment of the wicked is in entire harmony with the paternal character of God.* The argument will embrace the following propositions:

I. Our own nature, which is appealed to as refusing to recognize the attribute of punitive justice in a God of Love, in fact demands this attribute as essential to the moral perfection of the Deity,—an attribute without which He could not command the confidence and homage of his intelligent creatures.

* Prof. Tayler Lewis, in *Biblical Repository*, Sec. Series, Vol. X., p. 87.

II. The retributive forces continually at work in the natural world, and the punitive dealings of Providence with men, compel us either to admit that punitive justice is consistent in the Divine Being with paternal love, or to regard the head of Creation and of Providence as a tyrant.

III. The history of Israel, the chosen people of God, to whom he revealed himself as a Father, abounds in visitations upon them for their sins. If God has punished transgression in those to whom he was expressly revealed as a Father, he may punish the wicked hereafter, though he is a Father.

IV. Christ, who has so fully revealed God as a Father, teaches that God will punish the wicked in the future world; and we cannot claim his testimony upon the first point, unless we receive his testimony on the second also.

V. The high and sacred Fatherhood which the Gospel reveals, is a Fatherhood in Christ toward those who love Him; and not a general Fatherhood of indiscriminate love and blessing for the race. The same Jesus "who out of the fulness of an immeasurable trust called God Father," denied to the unbelieving Jews the use of that sacred name. Rejecting Christ's authority they said, " we have one Father, even God." Jesus said to them, " If God were your Father, ye would love me....Ye are of your father the Devil,"—quite another paternity.—" I speak that which I have seen with *my* Father, and ye do that which ye have seen with *your* Father." This distinction teaches that God is not the Father of those who have made themselves the children of the devil, in any sense which would exempt them from Christ's anticipative sentence, " Ye shall die in your sins."

VI. The demerit of sin demands that God should punish the sinner, if he would demonstrate his love for his intelligent creatures, and his care for the highest welfare of the moral universe ; and no punishment equal to the demerit of sin is, or can be, inflicted in the present life.

VII. Since this desert of punishment to the sinner, arises from that endowment of Free Agency which is essential to the attainment of that peculiar blessedness which is only within the reach of a moral being; and since the means of recovery from sin and of deliverance from condemnation can be made available only in the use of that same free agency of the sinner; and since the love of God has made the most ample provision of pardon, and has proffered this to the sinner with divine compassion and importunity, but only in vain;—there remains no conceivable mode, as there is no revealed promise, by which the Fatherhood of God can make one dying in impenitence and unbelief, holy and blessed in the future world.

VIII. The *duration* of the future punishment of the wicked cannot in any wise be limited by the mere fact of God's Fatherhood as made known in Christ; but must be determined by the demerit of sin, of which God alone can judge, and ascertained by us from the declarations of the Scriptures, which reason can interpret. The question of degrees of punishment is altogether secondary to the fact that, "he that believeth not the Son, shall not see life; but the wrath of God abideth on him."—The question of the annihilation of the wicked will be considered under this general head.

Before entering upon the discussion of the topics embraced in these propositions, let me premise a few words as to the spirit in which such a discussion should be conducted—

(1.) The investigation of a question so grave and momentous as that of the future state of the wicked, should not be entered upon in the spirit of controversy.—To controvert *error* is often needful for the establishing truth. The controversy of *opinion* upon secondary points in which good men differ, may tend to remove difficulties and to harmonize views. But the theme before us is one of infinite solemnity and of the weightiest personal import. Pugnacious controversy with error as such, should give place to kind and considerate, while cogent and earnest, argument with the errorist. Disputation about opinions as mere points of Orthodoxy, should give place to inquiry and persuasion touching interests personal and vital to all alike.

(2.) In such a discussion *dogmatism* is especially to be avoided.—What more offensive than zeal for the doctrine of Eternal Punishment, as a mere dogma of our own faith; a zeal that uses invective and denunciation against those who reject the doctrine, and that would seem almost to delight in having its assertions verified by the voice of some Dives crying from the place of torment; a zeal that would usurp the prerogative of the final Judge, and make religion consist only in terror! Far from us be such a spirit. Let not the preacher assuming his own safety, work out the logic of retribution upon others; but with the feeling of a sinner deserving all that he is authorized to denounce against iniquity, yet saved by that grace which he is commissioned to offer to all, let him " knowing the terror of the Lord *persuade* men,"—in Christ's stead " beseeching them to be reconciled to God."

(3.) Such a discussion should be conducted with the *sincerity* of a personal conviction of the truth maintained, not as an article to be defended but as a truth to be declared. "We believe and therefore speak."—If the doctrine of Eternal Punishment be true, it is easy to conceive of motives that would induce men to deny it, or to explain it away. I do not impute motives to any of the deniers of this doctrine, or impeach their sincerity;—but Human Nature, conscious of guilt and desert of punishment, is under a strong temptation to invent arguments against such a doctrine, to lend itself to sophistry, and to believe what it *wishes* to be true. This fact should subject that class of arguments to rigid scrutiny. But on the other hand we can conceive of no reason why an intelligent, humane, and conscientious person should *wish* to believe in the doctrine of Eternal Punishment if he did not find it in the plainest terms in the word of God. Priestcraft might invent a system of terrors whereby to rule the multitude. Superstition might invent such a system through an imagination excited by fear. But that an intelligent, humane, and conscientious person,—a mind like John Calvin, or Jonathan Edwards, or Timothy Dwight, or Nathaniel W. Taylor,—should hold such a doctrine without some strongly probable evidence of it in the Scriptures, is a fact that can hardly be explained by any theory of Human Nature, good or bad. Here is no selfish motive to originate such a doctrine, no darkened imagination to invent it, no ignorant fright to conjure up alarms. There is no pleasure in preaching such a doctrine; nay, it becomes tolerable to the pious heart, only in view of the glory of God's justice which it vindicates, and the glory of that grace which can deliver from so great condemnation. I do not preach this doctrine as a part of my theology, but as a part of the Savior's teachings. It should be preached with an honest desire to illustrate and enforce the whole truth of God. The minister cannot make his selection among revealed truths, but must proclaim each in its place. He may not withhold or modify any truth because it runs counter to men's tastes, or wishes, or prejudices; but must " declare the whole counsel of God, whether men will hear or forbear."

(4.) This doctrine should be discussed in the spirit of *humility*, with a reverent dependence upon the teachings of the Scriptures. It presents serious difficulties to a speculative and sensitive mind. Indeed, no candid and thoughtful person can fail to feel upon this subject difficulties like those which encompass the question of the existence of moral evil under the government of a holy and beneficent God. But we find greater difficulties in rejecting the doctrine of Eternal Punishment than in receiving it—difficulties both ethical and exegetical, which no ingenuity can set aside. The course dictated by sound philosophy in such a case, is to ascertain by fair principles of interpretation the exact teachings of the Scriptures upon the subject; and remembering that difficulties and objections in matters of faith do not necessarily imply that a doctrine is absurd, contradictory, or incredible, *to receive the clear and positive statements of the Scriptures as final*, even though we cannot free our minds entirely of the difficulties which those statements may excite. If a doctrine of the Scriptures could be shown to be contrary to reason, we must then reject not only that doctrine, but also the authority of the Scriptures as an inspired revelation.

(5.) The doctrine of eternal punishment should be preached in *the spirit of love*, with a view to the best good of mankind. Not for denunciation but for salvation, not for judgment but for mercy, should the preacher take upon his lips the awful declarations of the Bible concerning the final condemnation of the wicked. He should warn that he may persuade, should alarm that he may save.

It is as if we were upon a vessel laboring in a storm, shipping heavy seas and leaking in the hold; and as you were grouped together discussing the probabilities of her fate, I should come among you and say calmly but solemnly and earnestly, "The ship cannot survive. I have just come from a conference of her officers, and they say that she must go down:"—some might call me an alarmist, but the alarm would be prompted by the conviction of your danger, and the desire to save you; others might be thrown into a nervous fright, but the alarm would be addressed to reason and the instinct of self-preservation, not to mere animal fear. And if acting upon the warning of the officers I should betake myself to the life-boat, and thence should cry to you, "Sirs, the ship is sinking,—since I entered this boat she has settled an inch—*two* inches—*three* inches— she is sinking—make haste into the boat, she is *sinking*,—oh! do not linger!"—and saying this should throw you ropes and planks, and pass up ladders for your rescue—whatever you might think of my opinion, you would not question the sincerity of my conviction, the honesty of my purpose, the goodwill of my endeavor. And if believing the voice of the Master that there is danger of hell-fire, that men are sinking into everlasting wo, and believing this so much the more for having fled to Him for refuge, I cry out with words of warning and entreaty, they are not words of mere terror, nor of self-gratified assurance, but of real conviction, of earnest and beseeching love.

From this general outline of the argument, and these preliminary statements as to the spirit of the discussion, I now proceed to the first head to be considered.

I. *Our own nature which is appealed to as refusing to recognize the attribute of punitive justice in a God of love, in fact, demands this attribute as essential to the moral perfec-*

tion of the Deity—an attribute without which He could not command the confidence and homage of his intelligent creatures.

A frequent argument of objectors to the doctrine of future punishment is that our *nature* forbids us to conceive of a God who would make a hell for his creatures. The genial philanthropist already quoted says expressly, "We know that man's moral nature is good, and therefore that God is. Man is loving and merciful, and appreciates truth and equity. Goodness is natural to him." And from this he infers that God "has a just, forgiving, and loving spirit" toward his creatures. True, this philanthropist, who takes the most kindly view of human nature, is obliged to add that he would not infer the character of God from the actual characteristics of "the masses of men." He conceives of human nature in its normal condition and declares his "faith in its moral perceptions, and in its discernment, and appreciation of truth, justice and mercy;" from which he infers that "these qualities must all be found in the Author of human nature."

Doubtless there is a certain analogy between man and God; and in the strictly metaphysical sense, we can know God only as we know ourselves.* Our first conceptions of a Spiritual essence, endowed with intelligence, affections, emotions, will, must be derived from the facts of consciousness; and from the qualities of such essence as revealed within ourselves, we reason upward toward the Divine Nature. Paul reasoned thus at Athens: "Forasmuch as we are the offspring of God, we ought not to think that the Godhead is like to gold or silver, or stone, graven by art and man's device." We must reason from our own spiritual nature to that of God. The argument of Paul in the first two chapters of the epistle to the Romans proceeds upon this basis. While we cannot presume to measure the divine existence by our capacity of thought, and dare not transfer to

---

* Sir William Hamilton, Article on A Reform of the English Universities.

God the character of any man as it is, we are warranted in inferring the moral *qualities* of the Author of our nature from the constitution of the human soul in its normal state. The test proposed by our philanthropist is so far true ; and we do not shrink from applying it to the subject in hand. This very Nature which is said to revolt from the conception of a God of punitive justice, really demands this attribute as essential to the conception of God.

In studying our own Nature with a view to ascertain the moral qualities of the Divine Nature, we must bring our constitutional properties into equipoise, taking each into account, and in its just relation and proportion to all the rest. Grant, if you please, that our purely *Sentient* nature—which shrinks instinctively from suffering—may protest against the very thought of an eternal hell. Is Sensibility the whole of our Nature and the supreme judge of truth and equity, and even of the character of God? Does not sensibility shrink from pains and penalties inflicted by parental discipline and by human laws, which nevertheless are not "malignant and cruel," but salutary and good?

Grant, if you please, that our *Sympathetic* and *Emotive* nature is agitated by the thought of suffering inflicted upon others for whatever cause, and that humane sentiments and impulses of kindly feeling blindly assume that suffering thus inflicted must be cruel, and decry its author. Is this the whole of our Nature? Because my sympathies were stirred the other day by the cries and struggles of a woman whom the officers of justice were dragging to the Tombs,—so that I would fain have saved her from that shame,—does it follow that those officers were vindictive and cruel, and that under an administration of love and mercy there would be no prison for a thieving and drunken woman? Are there not other elements of our Nature beside its sympathies, to be consulted before deciding such a question?

Grant, if you please, that no *Intellectual* process of which we are capable can measure with mathematical certainty the connection between man's sin in this life and God's retributive justice in the Hereafter;—can Reason climb the height of this great argument so as to survey the wide extent of causes and results that lie open to the mind of God? Can Reason, fairly exercised, declare that the future punishment of the wicked is irreconcilable with the Divine Goodness? Though the reasoning faculty should insist that it finds no place for retributive justice in a fatherly Creator, is ratiocination the only process by which the soul comes to the knowledge of the right, the true, and the good? May not reason be perverted? May it not be over-confident? There remains another faculty, the *Conscience*, which on moral questions has the authority of law; and though this faculty is capable of being intensified and misdirected so as to rule the soul with a rod of iron, its place among the faculties is that of monitor and guide, and of a judge in matters of truth and equity. This Moral Sense and its decisions must be faithfully consulted in making up from the elements of human nature an estimate of the divine. If we would project from our own souls a positive likeness of God in his moral qualities, we must first photograph the negative with proper lights and shades, with a well-adjusted focus, so that no one feature shall be unduly magnified, but each shall appear in harmony with every other. And now when our Nature is questioned on the point whether God will punish sin, though Sensibility and Sympathy may shrink from the reply, and the Intellect may seek some negative subtlety, the Moral Sense replies, "He will punish sin, if his nature answers to that he has given to man; He must punish sin if man's own sense of right is to be satisfied; He must punish sin, if he would have the confidence, respect, and homage of moral beings made in his own image." The universal sentiment of mankind, that retributive justice is due to wrong doing—a feeling which God has implanted in the human soul—is a witness and a prophecy of His own righteous indignation against sin.

1. This sentiment appears in THE LAWS OF HUMAN SOCIETY. Grant what you will as to the injustice of many human laws—the tyranny of arbitrary power or of selfish exaction through forms of legislation; it yet remains that the basis of human law is the sense of justice in the soul—the discrimination which man's moral nature makes between right and wrong, between good and evil. And thus Law in its essential idea is an outward reflection of man's innermost consciousness, even as that consciousness in turn reflects herein the character and will of God; so that we need not abate one note of that magnificent pean of Hooker, "Of law there can be no less acknowledged, than that her seat is the bosom of God, her voice the harmony of the world; all things in heaven and earth do her homage, the very least as feeling her care, and the greatest as not exempted from her

power; both angels and men, and creatures of what condition soever, though each in different sort and manner, yet all with uniform consent, admiring her as the mother of their peace and joy."*

Law gives this stability and harmony without, this peace and joy within, only as it upholds Truth and Justice with penal sanctions commensurate with their worth. The rudest nations seek in some form to embody in law this inborn sentiment of Justice. It may be warped by prejudice or tinged with passion—as in the old demand of "blood for blood." It may mistake both as to its methods and its objects. To command assent, the outward expression of this sentiment in the form of law, must be guided by intelligence, and tempered with the humane and kindly feelings of the soul. But the sentiment is in our nature, and it cannot be rooted out. God has planted it there as a type of his own retributive justice.

This argument for the principle of retribu-

* Eccles. Polity, B. I.

tion in the divine government, derived from the infliction of justice by human society, was powerfully presented by one who witnessed the awful retributions of Society upon crime in California, in 1850. When the Vigilance Committee had done its needed work of expurgation, Dr. Bushnell, who chanced to be in San Francisco, preached a sermon suggested by the occasion, in which he urged these pertinent and emphatic questions:

"What kind of heaven would it make to move off bodily, into the eternal future, this same people just as they are? Just as good as it makes here, and no better. These revenges, frauds, bribes, perjuries and deeds of blood, these abuses of power, these factions, fears and tumults, all that makes you toss in throes of troubled apprehension, represents a character, as shadows do their substances. Who can imagine that out of such a material is to come order, love, ideal harmony, and the golden concert of a common joy before God? Why the irruption there of such a company would scare the angels from their songs, and extinguish the fires that light up the faces of the seraphim. When the Scriptures, therefore, declare that such shall not be admitted, what dignity of reason is there in the decree. And when it is published in solemn specification—'Be not deceived, neither fornicators, nor adulterers, nor thieves, nor covetous, nor drunkards, nor revilers, nor extortioners, shall inherit the kingdom of God'—who is there, even of those that are consciously named in the catalogue, that will not now, in this day of public misery, admit the necessary reason of the decree, and that even Eternal Goodness could not frame it otherwise?"

Were it announced that God would receive into a state of blessedness, with unchanged characters, the wretches whom men hunt out of human society by Vigilance Committees, could we honor Him as a Father or have confidence in his government? Should he say to the angels, all aghast at such a reeking blasphemous crew, "These creatures are my children, and therefore I have brought them to be with me in my glory"—could *they* revere and love the name of Father? Our nature demands a God the dignity and purity of whose love is not impaired by any effeminate weakness arising from the claim of *relationship*. Our Nature, which would not endure in a human judge that he should shield his son against the law, and interpose parental fondness between crime and its appropriate penalty, could not be satisfied with such a conception of God as the Infinite Father, nor look up to him with reverence, confidence and love. The profoundest philosophers and jurists of the pagan world have felt this necessary identity of justice in human law with justice in the mind of God.

" It is the pleasure of the gods," said Socrates, " that what is in conformity with justice should also be in conformity with the laws ;"* and often in his dialogues he maintained that in proportion as men cherish the sentiment of justice they are in harmony

---

* Xen. Mem. B. IV. C4. 25.

with the mind of the Supreme Divinity. Plato argues that to escape from evil one must fly to the seat of the gods; but this flight, he adds, "consists in as far as possible being made like to God; and this resemblance consists in becoming just and holy with wisdom.*....God is never in any respect unjust, but as just as possible, and there is not anything that resembles him more than the man amongst us who has likewise become as just as possible."†

Cicero, in his treatises on the Commonwealth and the Laws, argues the coincidence of the sentiment of justice underlying human laws with the principle of justice in the Divine Mind. "There is but one essential justice which cements society, and one law which establishes this justice. This law is right reason, which is the true rule of all commandments and prohibitions. Whoever neglects this law, whether written or unwritten, is necessarily unjust and wicked."‡ . . . .

---

* $\varphi\rho o\nu\acute{\eta}\sigma\epsilon\omega\varsigma$ Quere. A conscious aim? † Theætetus 84, 85.
‡ *De Legibus*, B. I.XV.

This, then, as it appears to me, has been the decision of the wisest philosophers—that law was neither a thing contrived by the genius of man, nor established by any decree of the people, but a certain eternal principle, which governs the entire universe, wisely commanding what is right and prohibiting what is wrong. Therefore they called that aboriginal and supreme law *the mind of God*, enjoining or forbidding each separate thing in accordance with reason. . . . The existence of moral obligation is coeternal with that of the divine mind. Therefore the true and supreme law, whose commands and prohibitions are equally authoritative, is the right reason of the Sovereign Jupiter."*

"True law is right reason confirmably to nature, universal, unchangeable, eternal, whose commands urge us to duty, and whose prohibitions restrain us from evil. Whether it enjoins or forbids, the good respect its injunctions, and the wicked treat them with indifference. This law cannot be contradicted

* De Legibus, B. 2. IV.

by any other law, and is not liable either to derogation or abrogation. Neither the senate nor the people can give us any dispensation for not obeying this universal law of justice. It needs no other expositor and interpreter than *our own conscience.* It is not one thing at Rome, and another at Athens, one thing to-day and another to-morrow; but in all times and nations this universal law must forever reign, eternal and imperishable. It is the sovereign master and emperor of all things. God himself is its author, its promulgator, its enforcer. And he who does not obey it flies from himself, and does violence to the very nature of man. And by so doing he will endure the severest penalties even if he avoid the other evils which are usually accounted punishments."*

2. THE RELIGIONS OF MANKIND give expression to the idea of Retributive Justice which conscience evokes in every human soul. Those strangely solemn pictures in the tombs of Egypt, which embody in vivid symbols the

* Commonwealth, B. 3, XXII.

religious ideas of the nation four thousand years ago, teach us that in the infancy of the human race, the moral sense of men led them to anticipate a retribution after death. You see the soul arraigned before the judge; the assessors ranged on either hand to note the trial; the sacred balances of justice suspended to weigh the actions or the heart of the deceased in one scale, by the figure or emblem of truth in the other; on this side the herald waiting to convey the approved into the abode of the gods, on that side the executioner waiting to lead forth the condemned. Not the Pharaoh himself could escape this scrutiny after death.

Osiris, whose worship was not confined as was that of some divinities to particular nomes or districts, but was observed from the earliest times throughout all Egypt, was represented under the favorite character of "the manifester of *good and truth;*" yet in that character "he was to every Egyptian the great judge of the dead!" The eye of Osiris is a frequent symbol upon Egyptian monuments, and upon mummy-cases and tombs is often found a group of hieroglyphics signifying "weighed in the balances," "weighed or tried by Osiris." Upon the tombs at Ghizeh is frequently found the epithet "weighed (and justified) by all the gods."* In the Egyptian mythology *Atum* or *Atmu* also has the functions of a judge in the lower world.

In the religion of Greece, the idea of a future retribution was continually prominent. The *Erinues* of Homer are the avengers of the moral order of the world against whoever may violate it. They frequently inflict punishment in this life, but they appear also in the hereafter, as the vindicators of eternal justice or the immutable Right. They are represented as walking in cloud, coming unseen to take vengeance upon the guilty,† and their vengeance reaches beyond the grave.‡

From the various epithets both of Greek and Roman mythology, designating *Jupiter* by his attributes, we learn that the god of the

---

* Wilkinson, Chapter 5.

† Il. 9. 571. 19, 87. ‡ Il. 19, 260. Od. 20, 78.

suppliant, and the god of mercy, was also the avenger of crime, the guardian of law, the protector of justice and virtue.

Themis appears as the personification of order, and her daughters have special charge over law and equity. One of them, Dike, the goddess of justice, holds in one hand a pair of balances and in the other a sword, and sternly awards to men according to their deserts.

But the most intense conception of retributive justice among the Greeks was in their *Nemesis*—the impersonation of divine wrath, the goddess of Retribution. The daughter of Night, silent, swift of foot, she hovers upon the track of the wrong-doer, pursuing him with certain vengeance. Aristotle describes Nemesis as a sacred jealousy, attributed to the gods that iniquity may be dealt with according to its deserts.*

The Romans had this element of retributive justice strongly, even terribly, personified in their mythology. In terrible conceptions of

* Rhet. B. 9.

the future they went beyond the Greeks, from whom they borrowed the ground-work of such pictures. Their *Tartarus*, with its hopeless bogs and flaming river, and the *Furies*, as ministers of vengeance upon the wicked, portray in glowing forms of terror the verdict of conscience against sin. Virgil, in the sixth book of the Æneid, distinctly describes Tartarus as a place of punishment for the wicked after death—a punishment lasting even to eternity. This woful prison with its triple walls, its flaming Phlegethon, its Furies, with snaky hair and whips of scorpions, pictures the punishment of guilt. Thus in almost every religion of antiquity, as now in the religions of the rudest pagan tribes, we find traces of this sense of retribution—especially in those expiatory sacrifices for sin which are co-eval with the history, and co-extensive with the dispersion of the race. No doubt this sentiment has often been perverted; and in rude and barbarous ages has been colored by the vindictive passions nourished in war. Divine justice has sometimes been only an exaggerated human revenge.—But still the grand, stern moral sentiment remains; the idea of Retribution, native to the human soul, has been incorporated with the religious beliefs of mankind. Who made the human conscience to utter this universal voice? Is the author of our nature who has caused the soul of man thus to cry out for the punishment of sin, a God who will forbear to punish because he is a Father?

3. If we turn from law and religion to LITERATURE, we find the same testimony. Paul tells us that " the Gentiles show the work of the law written in their hearts, their consciences also bearing witness, and their thoughts the meanwhile accusing or else excusing one another." And the writings of the great philosophers and poets of antiquity show that they had this consciousness of responsibility to law and liability to penalty. Take as examples, such leading men as Plato among philosophers, and Eschylus, the Shakespeare of the Greek tragedians. "We ought always to believe," says Plato, "those

ancient and sacred words which declare to us that the soul is immortal, that judges are appointed, and that they pass the highest sentences of condemnation, when the spirit is separate from the body."* Again he says, " When one supposes himself near the point of death, there enter into his soul fear and anxieties respecting things before unheeded. For then the old traditions concerning Hades, how those who in this life have been guilty of wrong, must there suffer the penalty of their crimes, torment his soul. He looks back upon his past life, and if he finds in the record many sins, like one starting from a frightful dream he is terrified and filled with foreboding fears."† Again in a sublimer strain, he thus apostrophizes the wicked. " Boast not of having escaped the justice of the gods; for thou shalt never be lost sight of by it. Thou art not so small as to hide in the depths of the earth, nor mounting on high shalt thou fly up to heaven; but

---

* Seventh Ep. to Dion.

† Rep. I. V. I have followed the condensed translation of this memorable passage by Prof. Tayler Lewis.

thou shalt receive thy due reward from the gods, either whilst thou stayest here, or in the realms of Hades, or carried to a place more wild than these."*

In the tenth book of the Republic, and also in Gorgias, Plato describes the wicked after death, as undergoing prolonged and terrible retribution; so that " to go to Hades with a soul full of crimes is the worst of all evils." He represents judgment as pronounced upon each *soul* apart, and as strictly awarding to the sinful soul the punishment that it deserves.

Plutarch in his vindication of Divine Providence from seeming neglect to punish the wicked, winds up the argument by an emphatic reference to a future retribution where justice will be meted out strictly to all.

But it is especially in the tragic poets of Greece, and pre-eminently in Eschylus, that we find this doctrine of future retribution, in its bearing upon the moral actions of men.

* Laws, X. 3.

> "Beneath the earth
> Great Hades holds his throne, the gloomy judge
> Of sinful men; and in his awful book—
> The soul's accusing conscience—reads their crimes."*

Again in a passage still more striking, the poet says, "The swiftly-turning balance of vindictive justice is ever ready to descend; to some in the broad light of day; for others, with lingering, accumulating force it awaits the dark twilight of life; for others is reserved the future, unending night."† The ideas of *delay* and *certainty* in the infliction of justice are often combined in the tragedies of Eschylus. Retribution, though it linger, is sure to come, here or hereafter. The law of retribution for the crime of murder is said to be as fixed as the divine existence. "It remains as long as Jove remains, that he who has done the deed must suffer; for it is an established law.

---

* Eumenides, 263-5. The above paraphrase is by Prof. Lewis. Prof. Hackett translates

> And all the deeds of mortal kind,
> He sees and writes them in *his* mind.

But the idea of a record is the same in both readings.
† Chœphorœ, 52-58.

(θεσμιον.)*" The doctrine of punishment for sin runs through all the theology of this greatest of classic tragedians. "Death is no escape, to the wicked, from their sins or the consequences of them. Their crimes will follow them into another world. The same Furies that pursue them on earth, unless appeased and reconciled, will follow them in Hades, nay, in Tartarus, which is their fit and favorite abode. In Hades also, there is a tribunal, which the wicked cannot escape, and a faithful record of their lives, and a just judge, who will certainly bring them to judgment and punish them according to their deeds."†

The Greek dramatist Sophocles, though less theological than Æschylus in the general cast of his tragedies—gives frequent expression to that doctrine of avenging justice with which the Greek mind was imbued. Hyllus, the son of Hercules, thus invokes the

---

* Agamemnon, 1540.
† Prof. Hackett on the "Theology of Æschylus." Bib. Sacra Vol. XVI. p. 399.

vengeance of the gods upon his mother, who had caused the agonizing death of the hero, by means of a poisoned robe, whose virus "shot anguish through all his bones."

> "Such were thy counsels, mother, such thy deeds
> To my poor father; for which traitorous acts
> May *penal justice* and the avenging Fury
> Meet recompense award thee. Thus I pray,
> If it be lawful—lawful it *must* be,
> Since every law towards me thyself hast spurned,
> And slain the best and bravest of mankind."*

In the Philoctetes the poet utters the sentiment that penal evil follows upon the violation of the constitution of the soul.

> All must be ill,
> When man the bias of his soul† forsakes,
> And does a deed unseemly. (902.)

In the *Ajax* we have the phrase, "the unforgetting *Erinys* and the fulfilling or unfailing *Dike*"‡—a retributive justice that never forgets and that never fails to accomplish its purpose.

In the Electra, which like the Choëphoræ

---

* *Trachiniæ* 809 seq.

† Τὴν αὑτοῦ φύσιν, Query—his *moral* nature—his conscience?

‡ Ajax 1389.

of Æschylus, and the Hamlet of Shakespeare, is a tragedy of retribution for the crime of murder, the poet brings out the doctrine that a god of justice reigns, and that notwithstanding the skepticism and despair of mortals in view of successful and seemingly prosperous crime, that justice "moves on tardily and stealthily, but surely to the infliction of the penalty upon the wicked."*

The chorus continually bring out this idea.

> Still in yon starry heaven supreme,
> Jove, all-beholding, all-directing, dwells.
> To him commit thy vengeance. (174)

Compare with this the counsel of the apostle—"avvenge not yourselves, but rather give place to wrath;"—refer the vindication of your character and your rights to divine justice —for " vengeance is *mine* ; I will repay, saith the Lord." (Rom. xii. 19.)

Again, to indicate the manifold agencies of retribution, the chorus sing,

> With many a foot of matchless speed
> With many a hand of deadly deed,

* See the fine analysis of the Theology of Sophocles by Prof. Tyler of Amherst College, in the Bib. Sacra for July, 1860.

> Erinys, veiled in ambush now,
> With brazen tread, shall track the foe. (488,)

Thus in every form the doctrine of retribution for sin both in this world and in the Hereafter, is taught by this great dramatist in the very height of Grecian culture. It is a doctrine which commends itself alike to "the æsthetic and the moral nature of man."

Even Euripedes, who represents the atheistic school of Greek tragedy, says that "in the end the good obtain their due, but the wicked, as they are by nature, will never fare well."*

Whence came such conceptions of a future state of retribution? Whence this almost universal idea of a judgment and a state of punishment in the Hereafter? Let those answer, who assert that this idea is contrary to reason and to the feelings of our nature. "Men are not fond of what is irrational for its own sake; they certainly do not love their own misery. Why have they thus cruelly tortured themselves for naught?

† Ion, 1020.

Why have they indulged in such terrific inventions of fancy? Why have they passed a sentence so unjustly severe on their own depravity?"*

Ah, it is because the *nature* that God has given us demands the punishment of wrong doers, that this doctrine of retribution has so infused itself into the legislation, the religion, the literature of the race. Is not that nature then a transcript of his own? Says Aristotle, "We *must* be pained, it is a necessity of our moral being, when the wicked do not suffer, as well as when the righteous are not rewarded. Wherefore we justly ascribe this feeling of indignation at wrong to God."

This is not a feeling of revenge. There is no personal malice in it. It is the demand of your nature that the right shall be vindicated; and the same feeling that leads you to rejoice when the wrong doer is come up with or the criminal caught, pronounces itself against your own transgressions.

"The moral reason and conscience in man,

---
* Prof. Tayler Lewis, Bib. Repository. Sec Ser., Vol. X. p 103.

having their counterpart and antithesis in the Deity, must, therefore, be regarded as indexes of Him, and particularly of what goes on in his being in relation to human sin and guilt. The calm consideration of man's ethical nature, and the unselfish organic remorse of his conscience, which are consequent upon his transgression of law, are effluences from that Being whose eyes devour all iniquity. The righteous indignation into which the judicial part of the human soul is stirred by sin, is the finite but *homogeneous* expression of that anger against moral evil which burns with an eternal intensity in the purity of the Divine Essence."*

Read the tragedy of Macbeth; and as you follow the usurper and the fiendish woman who goads him on from crime to crime, do you not suffer a disappointment at every new success of bloody treason? Does not your nature plant itself upon the side of right, and cry for vengeance? It is a relief when you come at last upon that terrible scene

---

* Prof. W. G. T. Shedd, Bib. Sacra., Vol. XVI. p. 731.

where the murderess, walking in her sleep, publishes her crime and groans with

"That perilous stuff which weighs upon her heart."

You breathe freely again when Macduff brings from the battle "the usurper's cursed head." You would not have it otherwise. Had Shakespeare left the wicked in his triumph, men would long ago have hissed him from the stage. Human nature demands that, even in fiction, retribution should follow on the heel of wrong. Much more in history. When the proud Tarquin, abusing the confidence and hospitality of his friend, enforced his passion against the virtue he could neither tempt nor conquer, and the yet chaste Lucretia, unwilling to survive the shame, stabbed herself before husband and brother, crying for revenge,—her noble form borne to the forum with this tale of wrong, roused all Rome to vengeance. From patrician and from plebian, from soldier and from slave, went forth the cry, "Down with the Tarquin— away with the tyrant from the earth." And as you read the story on the page of Livy, it kindles in your soul the same indignation, and you take up the echo of two thousand years, "Away with the tyrant from the earth!" It is the cry of our NATURE for injured innocence, for outraged virtue, for the weak and helpless and wronged, that crime may not go unpunished. *Your Father in heaven made you so to feel.* And has He no indignation at such crime—no retributive justice for such an oppressor? Nay; because he is a FATHER, and the helper of the fatherless, " he will break the arm of the wicked. He will be a refuge for the oppressed. When he maketh inquisition for blood, he remembereth them ; he forgetteth not the cry of the lowly." Our moral nature bears witness, that, He who made us thus to hate iniquity and demand its punishment, will " by no means clear the guilty."

We have thus taken this doctrine of future retribution to our own hearts to be tested ; and the nature that God has given us declares it is, it must be true. The sentiment of justice he has implanted within us argues the sublimer justice of his nature. The conscience that ever speaks within us, voices forth his infinite hatred of sin, and warns us of his righteous retribution. I might leave the question of a future retribution to your own nature as the interpreter of the divine. Ponder this question with the two beings who to you are the greatest in universe—your own soul and its Maker. As in the still night you hear the accusing voice of conscience, ask your Maker whether He hath not also a throne of judgment. As you feel the condemning pang of conscience, ask Him whether he hath not also a day of retribution. Nay rather, beseech Him for that mercy in Christ which alone can deliver you from the doom that conscience prophesies and fears. Make conscience at peace with God; for surely there is a world where conscience turned to Remorse,

"Still bids REMEMBER! and still cries TOO LATE!"

LECTURE II.

Future Retribution Argued from the course of Providence in this world.

Mat. 5 : 45. *He maketh his sun to rise on the evil and on the good, and sendeth rain on the just and on the unjust.*

Ps. 34 : 16. *The face of the Lord is against them that do evil, to cut off the remembrance of them from the earth.*

Ps. 145 : 9. *The Lord is good to all; and his tender mercies are over all his works.*

Romans 1 : 18. *For the wrath of God is revealed from heaven against all ungodliness and unrighteousness of men.*

These things are spoken of one and the same God. Both classes of sentiments are contained alike in both Testaments. Does the New Testament of mercy in Christ proclaim that God is a perfect Father, and in proof of this, point to the fact that "he maketh his sun to rise on the evil and on the good, and sendeth rain on the just and on the unjust?" The Old Testament also declares that "the Lord is good to all, and his tender mercies are over all his works." Did the Old Testament declare that "the face of the Lord is against them that do evil?" This was not a stern decree for a rude and barbarous age, to be abolished by a higher dispensation of love,—but the New Testament also declares that "the wrath of God is revealed from heaven against all ungodliness and unrighteousness of men;" it reaffirms these very words of the Psalmist; and in view of the course of Providence as illustrated in the history of Noah and Lot, it adds with emphasis, "the Lord knoweth how to deliver the godly out of trial, and to reserve the unjust to the day of judgment to be punished."* And this is the true reading of the character of

* 2 Peter ii : 9.

God, whether in nature or in revelation. He is good, he is compassionate, he is merciful, he is forbearing; and he is righteous, he is just, he is true, and he hates iniquity. The "equilibrium of the divine attributes," appears in this combination of seemingly opposite traits. The Bible does not present the character of God in the form of a systematic definition and arrangement of his attributes, but points us now to this feature of his character and now to that, leaving us to gather from these several rays, the full impression of God as He is. Thus the Bible interprets the character of God from the course of nature and of Providence, as a wise, holy and good moral governor, administering the world with supreme benevolence and a discriminating regard for holiness as the highest good.

No other view can harmonize these various declarations of Scripture, or the facts of human experience upon which they are based. The facts exist. There is good in the world, and there is evil. There is sunshine warming the earth into life, and ripening its kindly fruits. And there are torrid heats and blasting droughts, when "the earth lies parched, and the cattle die, and there is destruction and pestilence issuing as from the sun itself." There are genial showers, and fructifying rains that cause the trees to clap their hands and the valleys to shout for joy. And there are torrents that uproot the forests and lay waste the fields; floods that sweep away the harvests, and desolate the homes of men; lightning and hail and tempest, that in one brief moment destroy the work of years, and devour flocks and herds and families. There is the joy of birth, and the gloom and aching sorrow of death. There is the gush of gladsome life, the hum of insects, the song of birds, the mirth and music of unfettered hearts; and there is pain and moaning in the chamber of disease, in the hovel of want, and there are stifled sobs around the closing coffin, and there are new-made graves wet with scalding tears. The stars sing out their perpetual rhythm of peace and joy; and the winds wail and howl, as they scatter the leaves of summer and bring up the clouds and chill of winter. And not the seasons only, but the days as well mark this alternation. "Is there not the Night also, as well as the Day? How weak, and in the hands of what unknown powers, does man feel himself to be, when, deprived of light he looks, or strives to look, out into an infinite darkness? Is not the Night around him, is not Death before him?"*

And this evil which is in the world, in the workings of nature, in the whole course of affairs, cannot be subdued or controlled by human skill or power. Sometimes it comes with measured tread, foreseen but still inevitable, as when an iceberg bears down steadily upon the ship's course, and in the midnight watch is right athwart her bows. Sometimes evil breaks forth upon us at unawares, as when the Pestilence smites thousands in a city. Sometimes the evil comes in our most hopeful and joyous moods, just when our toils are ended and our plans about to be fulfilled; it

* Thorndale, p. 504.

comes often upon the very march of prosperity, sallying as it were from ambush, and striking deadly blows upon flank or rear while the main column of events moves forward in accordance with our desire. We build a gigantic steamship, stronger than the waves; mightier than the winds. We make her hull of iron, and her engines of hammered steel. We put into her a motive power equal to all demands of speed, and all contingencies of storm, strain or accident. For her the ocean shall roll no more; the leviathan shall glide upon it as on a sea of glass; and the fiercest gales shall be but feathery puffs to fan her sides, without once changing her course. The ambition of Xerxes, ridiculed for centuries, is now achieved; and man shall bind the ocean in chains. Years of toil, millions of money, are to be repaid with proud success, and the inventor who was derided when the monster hung motionless in its cradle, shall hear the applause of two continents proclaiming him master of the seas. The Leviathan goes forth adorned as a palace; a floating city built for ten thousand men; merchantmen and men-of-war dance like cockle-shells upon her waves; the sea makes way before her, and every promise of her builder is fulfilled. But hardly have the huzzas of her departure died away, when she comes into port crippled and torn; the very power that should make her invincible, has caused her iron ribs to quiver, has rent her costly cabins, and buried engineers and stokers in the ruins of girders, decks and bulkheads. But while her middle hold is filled with anguish and despair, her bow does not feel the shock; her screw works on; and her huge frame unbroken pursues its steady course. Just as the tidings of her disaster reach the capital, the head that planned and the hand that moulded her, in the very hour of anticipated triumph, are smitten with the paralysis of death.* And so the great ship wherever she shall go freighted with wealth and pleasure and power, shall bear the scars reminding us that man has not gained domin-

---

* The explosion on the Great Eastern and the death of her architect were reported a few days before the delivery of this Lecture.

ion over sorrow, but is still the prey of calamity and destruction. Even so this world of ours freighted with human hopes and plans and joys, moves onward in its appointed course; but ever and anon some exploding gas shaking its rocky ribs, brings down towers and hamlets; mountains pour forth rivers of fire, and seas roll in to bury cities; there is a cry of anguish, a burying of the dead; but the earth moves on in its accustomed track. There is evil upon it, there is evil within it, and man is like a passenger who walks upon a quivering deck, and sleeps beside a heated flue. There is danger; and we know not where to meet or how to shun it. There is evil, and we know not where it shall break forth upon us; or if we see it, we see also that its ministry is appointed, and that we cannot shake it off. There lies the fact; alike for atheist, unbeliever, pagan, Christian; the fact of calamity and suffering and woe and death inseparable from this world, which is so obviously and so largely planned for good. What does it teach us?

In my first lecture it was argued that the constitution of the human mind recognizes *punitive justice against iniquity* as the demand of moral Right and true Benevolence; and that in this feature the mind of man answers to the mind of his Creator. This moral sentiment of the race, demanding the punishment of wrong-doing, was shown to exist in the laws, the religions, and the literature of mankind in all ages and countries; and by its universality to prove that it was implanted by God, when He made man in his own image. Either then our own nature is " cruel and vindictive" when it cries out for the punishment of crime; either conscience when denouncing retribution upon sin is "a bloodthirsty tyrant" in the soul; or God is not vindictive and tyrannical when He threatens to punish sin, or when He does punish it according to his estimate of its enormity.

And now from this inner world of consciousness, where we have seen God reflected as it were face to face, and have found in our moral sense the witness and the prophecy of his retributive justice, we turn to the outer world of his creation and providence, and inquire what lessons this teaches as to the punishment of sin. My second general proposition is that,

II. *The retributive forces continually at work in the natural world, and the punitive dealings of Providence with men, compel us either to admit that punitive justice is consistent in the divine Being with paternal love, or to regard the head of Creation and of Providence as a tyrant.*

This proposition furnishes the only reasonable basis upon which we can harmonize in the character and plans of one perfect Being, the exuberance of good and the dark dread mystery of evil, in Nature and Providence.

Let us see what other modes of explanation have been offered.

(1.) First, there is the theory of Atheism, which regards evil as the product either of chance or of fate; and which argues from the very existence of evil, against the existence God. Thus Epicurus the leader of a school of Atheists among the Greeks, argued that "the world being imperfect, and presenting nothing but scenes of misery, destruction, and death, cannot be considered the work of an intelligent Cause." And David Hume in the defence which he puts into the mouth of Epicurus, and which is really the guise of his own skepticism, sneers at "all the fruitless industry to account for the ill appearances of nature, and save the honor of the gods; while we must acknowledge the reality of that evil and disorder with which the world so much abounds.".... And from this prevalence of evil, he denies "a Providence and supreme Governor of the world, who guides the course of events," and denies also a future state.* But even if we could thus get rid of a God from the universe, this would not help us to get rid of the evil. *That* remains in all its horror. God or no God, there still are earthquakes and tempests, and lightning and flood, and pestilence and death. *Nature*, which some make their divinity, Nature which some

* Works IV., 162–4.

adore as a loving mother, has all these terrors and woes, and leaves them unexplained. The so-called religion of Reason does not, cannot explain them. Neither chance nor fate can solve the mystery of evil, or lessen our weight of pain and fear.

Beside, the evil is too uniform and systematic for chance. It is not here and there a case of disease and death; but all men have pain and sickness, in some form, and all men die. And in certain cases there is a marked connection of cause and effect, and especially a connection of moral causes with physical sufferings—as when the drunkard suffers *delirium tremens*. These facts contradict the notion that evil comes by *Chance*.

And the frequent and obvious connection of physical suffering with moral transgression —as in "the social vice"—equally disproves the notion that evil comes by *Fate*, some blind eternal cause or law; for Fate cannot be presumed to act from an intelligent regard for moral causes. Yet we see acts which are moral in their origin and violations of a fundamental moral law, followed by physical pains and various temporal evils. Could Fate so ordain? Thus Atheism is tossed from horn to horn of its own dilemma—from Chance to Fate and Fate to Chance, till both are broken. Meanwhile the evil exists and may exist for ever; for why not some more horrible chance, some more direful and crushing fate in the future, than any yet experienced? It does not dry one tear of sorrow, does not relieve one pang of want, does not arrest or mitigate one symptom of disease; it does not take away the sting of death, nor light the darkness of the grave; it does not calm one apprehension for the future—to say there is no God.

Nay, Atheism throws us back into the darkness, the turbulence, and terror of chaos, where there is no Dove hovering with the olive branch of peace, no voice of the Almighty saying, "Let there be light," but that bird of evil omen, which the poet of Despair saw enter his chamber,

> Ghastly grim and ancient *Raven* wandering from the Nightly shore—
> And his eyes have all the seeming of a demon's that is dreaming,

And the lamp-light o'er him streaming throws his shadow on the floor;
And my soul from out that shadow that lies floating on the floor,
Shall be lifted—*nevermore*.

(2.) From Atheism we advance to Dualism —from the doctrine of no God to that of two gods dividing the empire of the world with conflicting interests and wills. This doctrine, which is as old as the Persian mythology, is that from eternity there have existed two opposing powers—the Lord of light, who is blessed in himself and beneficent toward all—and the Lord of darkness, who is miserable in himself, and malignant toward all. But thus to personify evil as a divinity, does not at all relieve the problem of our existence and destiny; nor does it afford any ground of confidence in the being of God. For if God be not the master of evil in the creation; if he does not hold it under his control; if it exists there without his consent and in conflict with his will and plan, in *every* sense; then since evil often seems to have the upper hand, since one hour of tempest, earthquake, fire, flood may destroy what months and years of beneficence have accomplished, what guaranty is there that evil will not triumph in the long run, that the lord of Darkness will not sweep the hopeless sons of men into eternal night and woe? If evil exists in the creation as an independent organic principle or power, which God himself has warred upon for six thousand years in vain, then there can be little hope for us in the thought that God is good. There stands the evil which He does not, and by this theory cannot overcome; and *we* may be crushed by that, though in respect to others God's plans of benevolence should prevail.

We can find no refuge from the idea of future retribution in a theory of the benevolence of God which separates Him absolutely from the authorship and control of natural evil. Homer habitually speaks of mortals as having a wretched, pitiable lot, and represents Jupiter himself as saying that "there is nothing more wretched than man among all things that live and move upon the earth;" *

* Iliad, xvii. 446.

through life "paramount in woe above all meaner creatures, and dying in a gloom unrelieved by hope."* Such must be the condition of man if the evils that are in the world are not under the control of divine wisdom and love, for moral ends.

(3.) A third theory proposed to meet these facts is, that the evil we here experience proceeds from God in the exercise of his mere sovereignty and arbitrary power, or through some mysterious plan in nature, but is in no way connected with a moral administration, dispensing evil as an admonition or reproof for the transgression of moral law. Such a theory has been maintained by Mr. Hume and other Deists, who would be willing to admit a Deity in the sense of "the Author of nature," but who deny a moral governor over the world.

A popular authoress presents this theory in all its force from the lips of one who is distracted with sorrow ; "I see everywhere a Being whose main ends seem to be beneficent,

* Gladstone, Homer, ii. 394.

but whose good purposes are worked out at terrible expense of suffering, and apparently by the total sacrifice of myriads of sensitive creatures. I see unflinching order, general good-will, but no sympathy, no mercy. Storms, earthquakes, volcanoes, sickness, death, go on without regarding us. Everywhere I see the most hopeless, unrelieved suffering—and for aught I see, it may be eternal. . . . Any father," she adds—and this is in the popular form of the argument—" any father who should make such use of power over his children as they say the Deity does with regard to us, would be looked upon as a monster by our very imperfect moral sense. Yet I cannot say that the facts are not so."*

If we conceive of God as merely using his *power* to produce evil, without an intelligent moral reason for such a use of his power, then we do make him a monster; and the very point of my argument is, that if you take away from your conception of God the idea of his punitive justice against sin, you make him

---

* Mrs. H. B. Stowe in the " Minister's Wooing."

a capricious tyrant in his administration over *this* world, using his power as only " a monster" would use it. If you deny that retribution for iniquity is consistent with the fatherly character of God, then there is no way of reconciling with that character the evils we find in the course of nature and of providence. Take away the moral reason for the infliction of evil which is given in the fact that God is displeased with men as sinners, and you leave only the arbitrary and capricious will of an infinite Power. There is no possible conception of God as a Father warranted by the facts of nature, which does not, in the evils he inflicts, recognize his moral nature in hostility to sin.

These evils are not arbitrary. Many of them, indeed, are mysterious, because lying beyond our ken. But others are clearly methodical, and for a moral purpose. This is obviously true of the large class of evils which flow directly and uniformly from vice. The want and disease, the shame and suffering which follow in the train of drunkenness and other forms of debauchery, are not casual or arbitrary inflictions of evil by a higher power. Such evils are inflicted by method, with an obvious design, and for a moral end. But arbitrary power does not act with the uniformity which reasonable and moral motives prescribe; and therefore since much of the evil inflicted upon men can be traced to such motives on the part of God, the fact that he inflicts evil does not prove that he is arbitrary or tyrannical; and therefore the fact that he threatens, and will inflict, other evils *hereafter*, is no more evidence against his goodness than is the fact of present evil inflicted by his hand. So far as the principle is concerned, both classes of evils, present and future, stand upon the same basis. If the infliction of evil upon transgressors in a future state of retribution is inconsistent with the benevolence of God, then the infliction of evil in this world proves that he is not benevolent. Here *are* evils, manifold and tremendous. If we can view these as connected with the *moral* government of God over an apostate and rebellious world, we can explain them without impeaching his benevolence; we can even find in them an argument for that benevolence, and "feel how awful goodness is." We can see also how to escape evil in the future by reconciling our characters with His. But if you take away from the divine administration this element of indignation at sin—if you deny that God is a moral governor—you are left in the midst of evils unexplained and unwarranted, and with no ground of hope that these will not be multiplied in another state of being. Take away the moral government of God, and you see no Father in the natural world. Creation and providence are a mystery, dark and foreboding. For He who would inflict such sufferings as we here endure, as mere demonstrations of his power, and without a justifying moral cause, is not a father but a tyrant. If the sovereign of the universe uses his power, as Louis Napoleon used his when he ordered the boulevards of Paris to be cannonaded, in order to inspire *terror*—if he conceals his purposes and smites at will for his own secret ends, then the thought of eternity can only fill us with dread. Rather let me live under the government of Him, who while he abhors iniquity, is a just God and a Saviour. It is vain to say that evil is only disciplinary, for much of the evil seen in the world has manifestly no such effect. And what of death? Is this always disciplinary to its immediate subject?

(4.) We come then to the only rational interpretation of evil as seen in the course of nature and of providence, and to its bearing on the argument for the retributive justice of God in the future state.

As we study the organization of nature and the administration of this world, we find a comprehensive plan; that plan in its manifest intent and far-reaching scope is benevolent; where evil exists, it is often a clear and unmistakable expression of God's moral purpose, approving virtue and condemning vice. We have reviewed and have dismissed as illogical and contrary to fact, the notion of Atheism whether of chance or of fate, the notion of

Dualism, or of two conflicting powers in the creation, and that notion of Deism which represents God as an infinite and arbitrary *Power*, acting by sheer sovereignty and not as a moral Governor of the world. Instead of such a world of disorder, of conflict, or of stern mystery, we find a plan, devised and ordered for beneficent ends. The course of nature and of providence is not by mere mechanical laws, but is animated as with a spirit of wisdom and benevolence so as to convey to us continually the expression of God's love. "The Lord is good to all, and his tender mercies are over all his works." Our Father in heaven "maketh his sun to rise on the evil and on the good, and sendeth rain on the just and on the unjust." I need not here multiply the proofs of the divine benevolence, for that is not now in dispute. Those whose opinions I am canvassing hold that God is good—*too* good to punish sin hereafter.

But with all the benevolence that God manifests in his works and ways, he also inflicts evil in such a manner as to show his disapprobation of sin. Bishop Butler calls attention to a fact in the course of Providence, which has never been disproved, and which cannot be gainsaid. That fact is, that " amid all the seeming mystery connected with the distribution of good and evil in this world, (and there is much about this which we cannot yet understand) so far as good and evil, happiness and misery are seen to depend upon the moral conduct of man, all *that* good is the effect of virtue, and all *that* evil is the effect of vice." Grant that the comparatively good suffer many evils; suffer more outward evil at times than do the grossly wicked. These good men, conscious of their own imperfection as compared with the standard of character, conscious of their own sins before God, never feel that they are treated worse than they deserve, or in any wise unjustly. The evils they suffer can never be traced to their *goodness;* nor do they suffer those inward smitings of conscience and pangs of remorse that make the wicked "like the troubled sea, which cannot rest."

On the other hand the wicked receive manifold providential favors. But these do not come as the natural fruit of wickedness. No man can claim the sanction of Providence for his crimes. The unequal distribution of good and evil under general laws, shows that this is not a world of strict retribution. The favors enjoyed by the wicked show that God here uses reclaiming influences with men. But we can still trace without mistake the whole tendency of his government, and his moral purpose in the infliction of evil. Evil does come often, manifestly, directly, terribly, as the consequence of sin. Every vicious man knows this. There are retributive forces in nature that declare war upon his sins. His own constitution warns him of the penalties of vice. And he carries within him an accusing, reproving, tormenting conscience, teaching him that sin and misery go together; and in the midst of his revels, debaucheries and blasphemies, writing upon the walls of his soul, in letters of fire, the warning of a judgment to come. So that amid all the beauty and beneficence of nature, and all the bounteous love of Providence, it still is true that "the face of the Lord is against them that do evil;" and that "the wrath of God is revealed from heaven against all ungodliness and unrighteousness of men."

Such evil so clearly marked against sin, cannot be treated as a mere discipline in the natural course of development for a moral being. Was Gabriel developed to his present position of moral perfection and glory by such process of physical suffering and such tortures of conscience? Have the angels of heaven been developed by any such experience of misery? Can we conceive of beings *morally* perfect as subjected by the Creator to suffering and fear, misery and remorse, as a means of development? Indeed if an experience of suffering is necessary to moral development, then the Creator himself is dependent upon the suffering caused by the sin of creatures for his own moral perfection! Nay, these facts of evil in our world belong not to the natural development of a state of existence, but to the fearful fact of *sin* which has brought upon man the just displeasure of God.

But these evils, terrible as they are, are not fully retributive. Their unequal distribution, and the fact that they are so exceeded by acts of kindness, prove that the full penalty of God's moral law is not yet meted out. Particular evils may be the penalty of physical and social laws, but we do not here behold the full equal measure of God's retribution. Yet we do trace the principles of his government, and read their warning. For while these present evils, rightly used, may be with some a means of discipline and reformation, they are *admonitory* and prophetic for all, concerning the principles of God's government—*a warning and a prophecy.* That Being whose goodness we behold in all his works, whose bounty we feed upon every day, whose love we rest in every night, the God " in whom we live and move and have our being," is unequivocally displeased at our transgressions. He shows that displeasure in the pains and sufferings that come upon us through the violation of *law*, whether physical or moral, and in the fears and forebodings of conscience for the future, that mingle with its upbraidings for the past. Guilt sees ever its own shadow as an avenger; and as the night of death draws on, and the sun of hope declines, that shadow grows colossal, darkening the soul. The evil felt augments the evil feared. The tokens of the divine displeasure at sin experienced in this world of abounding goodness and mercy, assure us that the God of love may also be "a consuming fire." It is not safe to take the risk of meeting Him as a transgressor. It is not safe to presume that He is too good to punish. It is not safe for a mortal to step forth over the chasm of death upon the cord of hope his own hands have twisted, with the weight of his sins upon his back, and no friendly hand to hold him. He may come under the cataract, his feet may slide, and no guy or balance-pole can arrest his fall. It is fool-hardy thus to presume upon the goodness of God. Good as He is, He is not too good to visit men here with tempest, lightning, earthquakes, fire and flood; good as He is, He is not too good to send upon the whole race disease and death. God is love, he doeth good to all. He maketh his sun to rise; "He sendeth rain upon the just and unjust;" and yet "before him goeth the pestilence and burning plagues are at his feet." Good as he is, the pathway of his providence is strown with warnings to the sinner, and the history of the race is dark with his retributive justice upon the wicked. He threatened the old world with a flood, and the flood came and destroyed them all. Does any man in his senses believe that the souls of those ancient rebels were borne up by the destroying waves to the heavenly glory, while righteous Noah was left to struggle on in a world of evil? Good as God is, He was not too good to threaten the guilty cities of the plain; and not all the pleading of Abraham his friend, could save them from destruction. "The Lord rained fire out of heaven and destroyed them all." Does any man in his senses believe that those devouring flames became chariots of fire to convey the spirits of the wicked to the skies, while Lot was left to toil and suffer here? Good as God is, He was not too good to visit Pharaoh and his land with plagues; to drown Pharaoh and his army in the sea. Does any man believe that the Egyptians were taken in glory to heaven, while the Israelites were kept sorrowing in the desert? Good as he is, He was not too good to terrify Beltshazzar at his feast with a warning of his doom, and " that night was Beltshazzar slain." Does any man in his senses believe that the sensual, daring, godless king was taken to heaven, and Daniel left to the hard fortunes of this life? Good as he is, He was not too good to destroy Jerusalem, bringing upon the heads of the Jewish nation the blood of his Son,—though Christ had wept over the city with the most exquisite tenderness of pity. Assyria and Egypt, Babylon and Tyre, Judea and her people, witness to God's righteous displeasure at sin. Have done with that sentimental fiction which some men call God, and look at God as He is.

"He tells you in a manner not to be mistaken, that he is displeased. He tells you in every painful thought, fear and misgiving, in every sting of anguish that conscience inflicts, in every evil which sin brings upon yourself and every sinner, in the sorrows, tears, woes and death of a groaning creation around you. .... All this he hath done and is doing. And is there nothing probable after death? Think of these things. Think of the question which death will decide in respect to yourself;—a question the mere uncertainty of whose decision is enough to convulse a universe with trembling. Is thoughtless sin then the wisest, safest, best preparation for meeting God in death? I say not what will be. I ask you only to think of what with fearful probability may be. Do you say you can meet it with composure, and drive away the forebodings of conscious guilt? I tell you no —not if reason remains and conscience lives. Nero had not firmness of nerve enough for this. Voltaire, with his settled deadly hate of Christianity, could not do it. There is a God. He hath given a law. That law to the guilty mind will bespeak a judge. The throne of heaven to the eye of conscience will be filled with a living, reigning, sin-avenging God."*

* Dr. N. W. Taylor.

LECTURE III.

FUTURE RETRIBUTION ARGUED FROM THE FATHERHOOD OF GOD IN CHRIST.

I Peter i : 17. *And if ye call on the Father, who without respect of persons judgeth according to every man's work, pass the time of your sojourning here in fear.*

Is God a *Father?* So Jesus taught us to say—" Our Father which art in heaven." But He is also a *Judge*, scrutinizing our daily conduct, and holding us to a strict accountability. He is the Father of Lights, and he governs the material universe by law. He is the Father of the spirits of all flesh, and he governs these by laws appropriate to their being. We have seen that the very constitution of the human soul, the offspring of God, made in his image, recognizes the fitness of retribution for sin, and requires this element of retributive justice in the head and ruler of the moral universe to satisfy its own sense of right. We have seen also that the physical evils of the present life stand connected with a moral system, and can be harmonized with the paternal goodness of God only as testifying his displeasure at sin. In other words, we cannot prove the perfect benevolence of God unless we conceive of him as a moral governor administering his providential government so as to testify his approbation of holiness, and his abhorrence of sin.

The Scriptures combine these two aspects of the divine Being,—the paternal and the judicial—in order to a just exhibition of the character of God. The course of thought in which the text occurs is most significant. The apostle addresses the disciples of Christ as "elect" or chosen "according to the foreknowledge of God the Father;" as having been begotten by the mercy of God the Father as the children of hope and heirs of salvation; as the loving and faithful disciples of Christ, rejoicing in Him "with joy unspeakable and full of glory;" and already by that living hope which Christ imparts, reaching forth and "receiving the end of their faith, the salvation of their souls." Surely such if any, are the children of God—having the warrant of faith, and of his adopting love and his indwelling spirit, to cry Abba, *Father*. Surely these are they to whom the Lord Almighty hath said, "I will receive you, and will be a Father to you, and ye shall be my sons and daughters." And yet the apostle charges them "as obedient children" to be holy, even as He who hath called them is holy. He bids them prove their filial relationship to God by forming a character like His; and reminding them that He who is their Father is also their judge, he charges them to walk before God with holy reverence. "If ye call on the Father," if you claim the holy God as your Father, then seeing that he is the righteous governor of the world, who spares none because of their professions, and is partial to none because of their filial relationship, but who "without respect of persons judgeth according to every man's work"—if you profess to be children of such a Father, "pass the time of your sojourning here in *fear*"—while in this world of temptation and sin maintain a deep and reverential feeling of your accountability to God.

As Archbishop Leighton describes it, this fear "is a holy self-suspicion and fear of offending God—not servile cowardice, but filial fear;—because you do call him Father, and profess yourselves his children, it becomes you, as obedient children, to stand in awe, and fear to offend him your Father, and a Father so full of goodness and tender love. But as He is the best Father, so consider that He is withal the greatest and justest Judge. He judges every man according to his work. . . . You profess the true religion and call him Father; but if you live devoid of his fear, and be disobedient children, he will not spare you because of that relation, but rather punish you the more severely. Because you pretended to be his children, and yet obeyed him not, therefore you shall find him your judge and an impartial judge of your works. Remember, therefore, that your Father is this judge, and fear to offend Him."

Language such as this addressed to those whom the Scriptures call the children of God, gives no warrant for the notion that because God is a Father he will not punish iniquity. In the same sentence we are reminded that God our Father is also our righteous Judge; and that we should walk before him with a reverential sense of our accountability. It behooves us therefore to consider in what sense the Scriptures hold forth God as a Father, and how this paternal character of God stands related to those attributes of moral and judicial sovereignty with which the Scriptures also invest Him. In considering this topic I shall dispose of the next three propositions of the original programme for these discourses.

III. My third proposition is that, *The history of Israel, the chosen people of God, to whom he revealed himself as a Father, abounds in visitations upon them for their sins.* If God has punished transgression in those to whom he was expressly revealed as a Father, He may punish the wicked hereafter, though he is a Father.

The paternal relation of God toward men has never been exhibited more strikingly than in his covenant with the house of Israel. The Lord called Abraham and separated him from the idolatrous community in which he lived, and constituted him the head of a nation as the chosen people of God. All the terms of parental endearment are lavished upon Israel in the name of the Lord, by the teachers and prophets whom he sent to declare his favor: "Jacob whom I have chosen"—"the seed of Abraham my friend"—"the Lord's portion is his people; Jacob is the lot of his inheritance. He found him in a desert land, and in the waste howling wilderness; he led him about, he instructed him, he kept him as the apple of his eye. As an eagle stirreth up her nest, fluttereth over her young, spreadeth abroad her wings, taketh them, beareth them on her wings; so the Lord alone did lead him, and there was no strange god with him." When Israel were in captivity, the Lord addressed to them these words of affection and comfort by the mouth of the prophet Isaiah: "thus saith the Lord that created thee, O Jacob, and he that formed thee, O Israel; fear not, for I have redeemed thee. I have called thee by my name—thou art mine. Fear not, for I am with thee; I will bring thy seed from the east, and gather thee from the west: I will say to the north, give up, and to the south, keep not back: bring my sons from far, and my daughters from the ends of the earth; even every one that is called by my name; for I have created him for my glory: I have formed him; yea I have made him." Indeed the Lord describes his love for Israel as transcending even the highest forms of earthly affection. "I am a father to Israel and Ephraim is my first-born." "Doubtless thou art our Father," exclaims the prophet, "though Abraham be ignorant of us, and Israel acknowledge us not;"— though our earthly progenitors, whose names we honor, do not know us as their children, though human lineage waxes old and dim with time, "thou, O Lord, art our Father, our Redeemer, thy name is from everlasting." And again with exquisite tenderness, the prophet represents Jehovah as saying to Zion, " Can a woman forget her sucking child, that she should not have compassion on the son of her womb ? Yea, they may forget, yet will I not forget thee. Behold, I have graven thee upon the palms of my hands; thy walls are continually before me." Could anything in human language express more of tenderness, of gentleness, and of faithful and patient love than is conveyed by these words? All that we can conceive of affection, of patience, of forbearance, of devotion in the feelings and relations of God to men, is conveyed in the declarations of the infinite Jehovah to his chosen people Israel. And yet in the very beginning of this peculiar relationship, when God constituted the nation under his own headship, and made his covenant of love, He revealed as well his attributes of righteousness and justice—his hatred of iniquity. "The Lord thy God hath chosen thee to be a special people unto himself, above all people that are upon the face of the earth. The Lord did not set his love upon you, nor choose you, because ye were more in number than any people; for ye were the fewest of all people. But because the Lord loved you, and because he would keep the oath which he had sworn to your fathers, hath the Lord brought you out with a mighty hand, and redeemed you out of the house of bondage, from the hand of Pharaoh king of Egypt. Know, therefore, that the Lord thy God, he is God, the faithful God, which keepeth covenant and mercy with them that love him and keep his commandments to a thousand generations, and *repayeth them that hate him to their face, to destroy them:* he will not be slack to him that hateth him, he will repay him to his face. Thou shalt therefore keep the commandments, and the statutes, and the judgments which

I have commanded thee this day, to do them." Thus in the self-same covenant in which God revealed himself as the Father of Israel, he also proclaimed himself a moral governor, declared his indignation at sin, and threatened his judgments upon the transgressor.

How faithfully this aspect of his character was displayed, the whole history of Israel will testify. How often were the heathen round about them used as a scourge to visit upon Israel the displeasure of God at their transgressions. How often did desolating war, and famine and pestilence bring upon them the judgments of the Lord. These calamities which might else have been ascribed to the ordinary course of nature, were specifically threatened as visitations from God because of the sins of his chosen. Even in the wilderness he showed his displeasure at the sins of his people whom he was leading as a flock. How many were destroyed because of the golden calf at Sinai; how many died of the plague because they murmured at their food;

how many fell a prey to war because they inclined to idolatry; and at last as a judgment from God upon their disobedience and unbelief, not one of the adult generation that came out of Egypt, save only Caleb and Joshua, was permitted to enter the promised land. Again and again the Philistines and the Amorites, the kings of Egypt, of Babylon, and of Assyria, were suffered to invade Judea, to ravage the country, to besiege the capital, to exact tribute, to carry away captives, and all this as a retribution from God because of the sins of the people. At length the whole nation was carried away into captivity—the ten tribes into Assyria, Judah and Benjamin to Babylon—Jerusalem was burned and the temple was destroyed. When after seventy years of captivity, the Babylonish exiles were restored to the land of their fathers, and suffered again to become a nation, they held their national independence and their heritage in the soil, by the tenure of obedience to God; and when again they rebelled, the Macedonian and the Roman came to execute his judgments. It cannot be said that these were the ordinary viscissitudes of a nation; the changing fortunes of war. These successive evils were *threatened;* they were predicted with minute detail; threatened because of sin, as a direct infliction from the hand of God. There is no evading this lesson of Jewish history. The government of that people was a type of God's moral government over the world; and the principle of retributive visitation for iniquity is written there for our instruction and admonition. What then? Did Jehovah grow weary of his people? Did he forget his promises of mercy, his paternal love, and become a stern and arbitrary sovereign? Nay; in these very dispensations of judgment we see the Father's heart melting with pity over the wayward and guilty people. "O Ephraim, what shall I do unto thee? O Judah, what shall I do unto thee? for your goodness is as a morning cloud, and as the early dew it goeth away." "How shall I give thee up, Ephraim? how shall I deliver thee, Israel? how shall I make thee as Admah? how shall I set thee as Zeboim—those doomed cities of the plain—mine heart is turned within me, my repentings are kindled together. I will not exeute the fierceness of mine anger, I will not return to destroy Ephraim." Thus once and again the father's love restrains the threatened judgment. But when the people unmindful of that love, go on to multiply transgressions, the same benignant and forbearing God—the same Father whose heart we have seen yearning over his children, declares, "Shall I not visit for these things? shall not my soul be avenged on such a nation as this? I will make Jerusalem heaps, and a den of dragons; and I will make the cities of Judah desolate, without an inhabitant; because they have forsaken my law which I set before them, and have not obeyed my voice, neither walked therein;" a Father still, and yet a God who will punish sin even in his children.

Will it be said that all these were judgments upon the nation as a whole, that they finished the work of retribution in this world, and therefore argue nothing for retribution upon individuals in the hereafter? I answer first, that judgments upon nations for organic or political sins must needs take effect in the present world; since it is only here that the nation exists and can be reached in its organic character. But secondly, what men do in a social and collective capacity they are responsible for also as individuals up to the measure of their personal agency. The Sepoy mutineers were disbanded and disgraced, and thus the troops in their organic character were punished; but their ringleaders were also hung or shot because of their individual treason which used the army organization as its agent. The judgments that come upon men in their collective capacity for public sins, do not fill up the measure of retribution for the individual partakers in those sins. It cannot be held to release one from personal responsibility, that he plans and contrives to do wickedly through some social or corporate organization.

And thirdly, I answer, that I am now combating the notion that the judicial punishment of sin is inconsistent with the character of God as a Father. And surely if the infliction of such punishment be inconsistent with the paternal character of God, it is just as inconsistent to punish men collectively as to punish them severally. If it was inconsistent with the paternal character of God to cause the earth to open a fiery pit and to swallow up Korah, Dathan, and Abiram, for making a mock of the priestly office, it was equally inconsistent with that character for the Lord to cut off fifteen thousand of the congregation by a plague because of their murmuring. The principle is the same in both cases. The collective judgment in this respect must be tested by the same rules we would apply to a judgment upon an individual. If one is unpaternal and vindictive, so is the other. But God who was the Father of Israel, and who gave all possible evidence of paternal love, *did* punish the people for their sins.

And again: In his dealings with Israel as a people, the Lord did visit individuals with special and signal marks of his displeasure at sin. Can any one read the history of Saul, of Ahab and Jezebel, of Joram, of Zedekiah, and deny that God will visit *persons* as well as nations for their sins? These kings did not suffer merely in those national calamities which came upon the people in their time. Judgments were threatened against them as individuals, because of their personal transgressions; and in all the history of Israel the principle of retributive justice upon individuals as well as communities is most clearly seen. But was not God then a Father?

And finally, in reply to the objection that the judgments upon Israel, being national, spent their force in this world, and argue nothing for future retribution,—I answer that if these be not an example and a prophecy with respect to the grand principle of retribution under the government of God, then such visitations are *meaningless* for any moral purpose—or worse than meaningless, they are a pretense of government without its power. Suppose that the children of Israel could have seen Korah and his godless crew emerging from the fiery pit that had swallowed them, and transported to the sphere of angels and of everlasting glory. What moral effect could the earthquake and fire have had upon the congregation? Suppose their conception of God as a Father had required them to believe that there would be no punishment for sin hereafter? What a stupendous *sham* in government would have been those judgments which gave the sinner a moment's pain to expedite his entrance into bliss. Suppose that when that wretch Jezebel was thrown out of the window to be devoured by dogs, the bystanders could have seen the veil of the spirit-world removed, and a convoy of angels with harps and palms and crowns, waiting to escort the murderess to Abraham's bosom. What must have been the moral impression of a judgment relieved by such a consequence! What the moral teaching of a theology that limits God's retributive justice against iniquity by the boundary of death! Far from this is the teaching of the Bible from these lessons of providential retribution. The apostle Paul, after enumerating the judgments of God upon Israel in the wilderness, adds, "Now all these things happened to them as ensamples," literally as types—expressive signs to the world of the principles of God's government; and "they are written for our admonition, upon whom the ends of the world are come." So Peter declares that Sodom and Gomorrah were destroyed as an example to those that after should live ungodly, an example "not so much *for* their warning as *of* their doom." So Jude declares that those cities of the plain are "set forth for an example suffering the vengeance of eternal fire." The punishment that befell their guilty inhabitants here, was but a beginning which hath no end, and a type of the punishment of the ungodly in the future world. *This* is the lesson of God's punitive dealings with men in this life; this the solemn lesson of his judgments upon the Jews. He was their Father, and He was their judge.

When at length the cup of their iniquity

was full, and with a horrid curse invoking his blood upon themselves and their children, they crucified the Son of God, then though Jesus himself had wept over the city and died to save its guilty inhabitants, though with his latest breath he cried "Father, forgive them," yet the judgment came; Jerusalem was destroyed and the nation scattered into captivity and exile. God their Father, "who without respect of persons judgeth according to every man's work," vindicated his moral government in their doom.

IV. The fourth position taken was that *Christ who has so fully revealed God as a Father, teaches that God will punish the wicked in the future world; and we cannot claim his testimony upon the first point, unless we receive his testimony on the second also.* It is sometimes attempted to set off the New Testament against the Old as being more mild and favorable in its presentation of God. It is alleged that the Jewish economy of law was for an ignorant and barbarous age, needing the restraints of penalty; but that

Christ has revealed God under another aspect—that of paternal love,—and that since Christ has taught us to call God our Father, we may dispel all apprehension of his punitive wrath. But if the Lord Jesus Christ is to be our witness in this matter, surely we are bound to receive his *whole* testimony, and to take the character of God in every point just as He has presented it. Let us therefore cite the words of Christ himself upon the question whether transgressors shall be punished hereafter under the government of his Father, and that mediatorial government which the Father has established through the Son.

"Except your righteousness shall exceed the righteousness of the scribes and Pharisees, ye shall in no case enter into the kingdom of heaven."

"Whoso shall say to his brother Thou fool, shall be in danger of hell fire."

"Enter ye in at the strait gate; for wide is the gate, and broad is the way, that leadeth to destruction, and many there be which go in thereat."

"Not every one that saith to me Lord, Lord, shall enter into the kingdom of heaven; but he that doeth the will of my Father which is in heaven. Many will say to me in that day, Lord, Lord, have we not prophesied in thy name? and in thy name cast out devils? and in thy name done many wonderful works? And then will I profess unto them I never knew you. Depart from me, ye that work iniquity."

"Thou Capernaum which art exalted to heaven, shalt be brought down to hell. It shall be more tolerable for the land of Sodom, in the day of judgment, than for thee."

"I forewarn you whom ye shall fear. Fear him, which, after he hath killed, hath power to cast into hell."

"As the tares are gathered and burned in the fire, so shall it be in the end of this world. The Son of Man shall send forth his angels, and they shall gather out of his kingdom all things that offend, and *them which do iniquity;* and shall cast *them* into a furnace of fire: *there shall be wailing and gnashing of teeth.*

Then shall *the righteous* shine forth as the sun in the kingdom of *their Father.*"

"Whosoever shall deny me before men, him will I also deny before my Father which is in heaven."

"For what is a man profited, if he shall gain the whole world, and lose his own soul? Or what shall a man give in exchange for his soul?"

"For the Son of Man shall come in the glory of his Father, with his angels; and then he shall reward every man according to his works."

"It is better for thee to enter into life halt or maimed, rather than having two hands or two feet to be cast into everlasting fire."

"And the lord of that wicked servant was wroth, and *delivered him to the tormentors,* till he should pay all that was due to him; *so likewise* shall my heavenly *Father* do also to you, if ye from your hearts forgive not every one his brother their trespasses."

"There shall be weeping and gnashing of teeth, when ye shall see Abraham and Isaac and Jacob and all the prophets in the kingdom of God, and you yourselves thrust out."

"The rich man also died, and was buried; and in hell he lifted up his eyes, being in torments."

"Ye serpents, ye generation of vipers, how can ye escape the damnation of hell."

"Then shall the king say to them on his right hand, Come ye *blessed of my Father*, inherit the kingdom prepared for you from the foundation of the world. Then shall he say also unto them on the left hand, *Depart from me, ye cursed, into everlasting fire*, prepared for the devil and his angels: and these shall go away into everlasting punishment; but the righteous into life eternal."*

Every one of these words was spoken by Christ himself. Did he not teach that there will be hereafter a distinction of condition grounded upon distinction of character here? Did not Christ teach that there will be a day of judgment and of retribution? Did not

---

* The reader is advised to trace these several passages, in their order, through the Gospels.

Christ teach that there is a hell? Did not Christ teach that the wicked shall be punished? Did He not teach that their punishment shall be eternal—that it shall endure as long as the life and blessedness of the righteous? And was not Jesus full of tenderness and compassion? Did he not die to save men,—and yet did not he teach that if they would not accept his grace they must die in their sins, and perish forever? No man knoweth the Father but the Son, and he to whom the Son revealeth Him. And how has Christ revealed God to us? Under that sentimental and poetic image which represents him as indifferent to sin, as so full of tenderness and compassion for suffering that he will not inflict punishment? Nay; nay; God is a Father, who that he might save us from sin and death, spared not his own Son. God is a Father who when that Son stood in our stead, would not take away from him the cup of wo in Gethsemane, and did hide his face from the beseeching agony of Jesus on the cross. Did Christ once doubt that God is a

Father? Did Christ once say that that Father will not punish sin? Ah, could these heavens open and we hear the Son of God proclaim the words that I have cited from his lips, what awe would they strike through our souls. Go alone, and read aloud this testimony of the Son to the justice and the punitive wrath of his Father.

In summing up the Bible view upon this point, it only remains to add a word upon the fifth proposition, viz:

V. *The high and sacred Fatherhood which the Gospel reveals, is a Fatherhood in Christ towards those who love Him, and not a general Fatherhood of indiscriminate love and blessing for the race.*

There is a general sense in which God is styled the Father of mankind; viz: as the author of their being and the providential supporter of life. In this sense also he is said to be the Father of *lights*—the author and head of the physical creation; and the Father of all creatures, as well as of the spirits of all flesh.

God is spoken of also, as the Father of men, because in their spiritual constitution they are made in his image. Hence the apostle James says of the tongue, "Therewith bless we God even the Father; and therewith curse we men which are made after the similitude of God."* But this general use of the term Father, to denote the author and supporter of life, does not carry with it those ideas of special kindness or parental favoritism, which some associate with the name. The privileges and promises which spring from the divine Fatherhood are pledged to those who by their personal character, as formed by divine grace, are brought into a special relation of filial love and obedience. Christ taught his *disciples* to pray "Our Father." Jesus said, "I am the way, and the truth, and the life. No man cometh to the Father but by me."† In his last conversation with his disciples before the crucifixion, Jesus forewarned them that the world would persecute them as his followers. "And these things will they do unto

* Jas. iii: 9. † John xiv: 6.

you, because they have not known the Father, nor me." But he adds, " the Father himself loveth you, because ye have loved me, and have believed that I came out from God." Thus he makes their faith in himself the means of introducing them into a filial relation toward God which the world knows nothing of. In his prayer he said, " O righteous Father, the world hath not known thee. I pray not for the world,"—in this consecrating prayer which set apart his own household of faith—" I pray not for the world at large, but for them which thou hast given me ; for *they are thine;* holy Father keep through thine own name those whom thou hast given me."*

Thenceforth in the New Testament God is spoken of as the Father of believers, in a high and sacred sense in which the world cannot share. Into renewed and believing souls He sends forth his Spirit crying Abba, Father. This filial relationship is always conditioned upon the renunciation of the world; upon a

* John xvi & xvii.

holy character begun by faith in Christ. "Come out and be ye separate saith the Lord, and touch not the unclean thing, and I will receive you; and will be a Father unto you, and ye shall be my sons and daughters saith the Lord Almighty."* Such a promise as this, expressly conditioned upon the renunciation of sin, upon the Christian type of character, conveys no immunities to the world at large. If they will comply with the condition they can enter into this blessed relation; but if not, they can hope nothing from the Fatherhood of God. The apostle John declares, "if any man love the world, the love of the Father is not in him;"† he is not in this filial relation with God. And Jesus said, "He that hateth me, hateth my Father also."‡

To recall what was said on this point in a previous discourse,—when the unbelieving Jews appealed to God as their Father, Christ denied their right to that endearing term. First they insisted upon their descent from

---

* 2 Cor. vi : 17.   † 1 John ii : 15.   ‡ John xv : 23.

Abraham as making sure to them the kingdom of heaven. Jesus answered, "I know that ye are Abraham's *seed;*—but if ye were Abraham's *children,* ye would do the works of Abraham."* The true lineage of Abraham is the lineage of faith. The fact that Abraham was their progenitor, could not of itself entitle them to the blessings of the covenant. He is the father of the faithful—a relationship established by *moral* resemblance. Dives, though a Jew, of the seed of Abraham, lifted up his eyes in hell, and saw Abraham afar off, and cried Father Abraham have mercy on me. But Abraham answered, " between me and you there is a great gulf fixed." Just so of the Fatherhood of God himself. The mere fact that we are his offspring does not ensure to us the covenanted blessings of his kingdom. We must be his children in character. When these same unbelieving Jews said tauntingly to Jesus, "We have one Father, even God"—Jesus answered, "if God *were your* Father, ye

* John viii · 37, 39.

would love me; ye are of *your father the Devil*, and the lusts of your father ye will do. He that is of God heareth God's words; ye therefore hear them not because ye are not of God."† And now in face of such clear distinctions, such solemn and emphatic declarations, can a man claim anything, hope anything from the gracious Fatherhood of God, unless he becomes a child of God by renouncing sin, and accepting Christ? Nay, "if ye call on the Father, who without respect of persons judgeth according to every man's work, pass the time of your sojourning here *in fear.* " The very Fatherhood of God toward us, conditioned as this is upon our holy affection toward him, is fitted to inspire us with reverence. The loving Father of believers is the impartial Judge of all.

That God threatens offenders with his displeasure no candid reader of the Bible will deny. Would he threaten if he meant nothing? If he threatens will he not keep his word? If his gracious Fatherhood does not

† John viii: 42, 44.

forbid him to threaten wrong-doers with his displeasure, neither will it forbid him to execute that displeasure when, without respect of persons, he shall judge every man according to his work.

1. Those who regard themselves as the children of God's adopting Grace, should be careful to honor his holiness by watching against sin in themselves, and by maintaining the truth in regard to his hatred of iniquity. " A son honoreth his father and a servant his master: if then I be a father, where is mine honor? if I be a master, where is my fear? saith the Lord of hosts to you, O priests, that despise my name. Cursed be the deceiver, who hath in his flock a male, groweth and sacrificeth to the Lord a corrupt thing; for I am a great king, saith the Lord of hosts, and my name is dreadful among the heathen."* Those who call themselves the children of God should take heed that his name is not dishonored through the imputation of a senti-

* Mal. i : 6.

mental effeminacy to his character, or through their failure to vindicate his justice. As the Bible does not soften its speech to "ears polite," neither should they who speak for God keep back or mutilate his testimony. It is a cheap and easy liberality to say " We do not *know* what shall befall the wicked hereafter, but leave that to God." A true apostolic love declares, that " *knowing* the ter-Lord, we *persuade* men."

2. Those who will not make God their Father by accepting his grace in Jesus Christ, must meet him hereafter only as their Judge. God *is* a Father to as many as come to him through Christ. He will be your Father, if you will penitently and truly seek his grace. But he judgeth all men without respect of persons; and they who are not reconciled in Christ, and made the children of adoption, can have no claim upon the rejected benignity of the Father against the impartial scrutiny and the inflexible decision of the Judge. "God is love"—" Our God is a consuming fire."

LECTURE IV.

FUTURE RETRIBUTION ARGUED FROM THE DE-
MERIT OF SIN.

Romans vi : 23. *For the wages of sin is death; but the gift of God is eternal life through Jesus Christ our Lord.*

IN the course of the argument thus far, we have seen that God has so constituted us in his image that our moral nature demands retributive justice upon wrong doing; and that the universality of this moral sentiment of the race fore-tokens the righteous retribution of God upon transgressors. We have seen also, that the Providential Administration of this world clearly reveals to us God's displeasure at sin, and the principle of retribution under his moral government. And, further, that as the *Father* of Israel, his chosen people, God did punish them for their iniquities, not only in their corporate capacity as a nation, but as individuals also, visiting them with judgments which were but a type of the retributions of the future state; that Christ who so fully revealed God in the tender relation of a Father, proclaimed with equal fullness the punitive wrath of God against sin, and the eternal punishment of the wicked; and that the Fatherhood of God which the Gospel teaches, has reference only to those who by faith in Christ become the children of his adopting love.

I now advance to the sixth general proposition; *to wit*—

VI. *The demerit of sin demands that God should punish the sinner, if He would demonstrate his love for his intelligent creatures, and his care for the highest welfare of the moral universe: and no punishment equal to the demerit of sin is, or can be, inflicted in the present life.*

Upon what ground does God threaten to

punish sin? Upon what ground must we rest the fact of punishment, to make it consistent with his benevolence?

That God does *threaten* to punish transgressors cannot be denied—as I have already said—by any who acknowledge the Bible to be his word. The Bible warns us of a judgment to come; the Bible warns us of the danger of losing the soul; the Bible warns us of a "hell," a "lake of fire," where "the worm dieth not and the fire is not quenched;" the Bible arrays before us the dread scenery of that Day when "the Lord Jesus shall be revealed from heaven with his mighty angels, in flaming fire taking vengeance on them that know not God, and that obey not the gospel of our Lord Jesus Christ: who shall be punished with everlasting destruction from the presence of the Lord, and from the glory of his power."* These things are *in the Bible*—with all this strength of expression. Great have been the labor and ingenuity expended in the attempt to

---

* 1 Thess. i: 8, 9.

tone down such language or to explain it away. But why is such language there at all? If it is inconsistent with the character of God as a Father to punish transgressors for their sins, is it not quite as inconsistent with Fatherly love to threaten to punish them if he has no thought of doing so? Does a wise and kind Father get up bugbears to frighten his children? Will he take them out in the dark night and shake them over a pit, either to terrify them into obedience, or to satisfy them that though he is so strong and could destroy them if he would, yet he loves them too well to do it? We think it good ground for dismissing a child's-nurse if she excites his imagination with idle threats and fears. And will parental love thus trifle with a child? Will a wise and kind Father govern his household upon such a system? And will the Father of all mercies daily mock the fears of his children with words of threatening and images of terror?

God does say in this book, that "he that

believeth not the Son shall not see life ; but the wrath of God abideth on him."* God does say in this book, that " he that believeth not shall be damned."† God does say in this book, that there shall be " a day of judgment and perdition of ungodly men."‡ God does say in this book, that " the dead shall stand before Him, and shall be judged every man according to their works ;" and that " whosoever is not found written in the book of life, shall be cast into the lake of fire."§ We can conceive of nothing in the way of threatening more appalling than these words. Is there then no reality corresponding with these threatenings from the lips of Almighty God? If you can prove that there is none, of what avail are they as threatenings? And what confidence can you have in a Being who seeks to terrify you with such idle threatenings—who feigns anger, who gets up all these words and images of terror to scare his creatures ? What must you think of the veracity of such a being? What of his hon-

* John iii : 36   † Mark xvi : 16   ‡ 2 Pet. iii : 7.   § Rev. xx : 13, 14.

esty? What of his wisdom? What of his kindness? Does the Father of mankind fill their consciences with dreadful forebodings of evil—make death terrible, and kindle along the verge of the future a lurid flame shaped into

"Gorgons, and Hydras, and Chimeras dire"—

and all for no cause in themselves, and no purpose in his moral government? Is that "our Father?" Nay, my friends, these fearful declarations of God's word can be made to harmonize with his benevolence only upon the supposition that there is something in the character of man as a moral being, in his relations to the government of God, which *deserves* all the evil that God has threatened.

The very preacher whom I quoted in the first lecture as teaching that punitive wrath is incompatible with paternal love, in his eulogy upon Theodore Parker, thus vindicates that austere and denunciatory critic and reformer, from the charge of being bitter, malignant, and vindictive. "When charity becomes intensest, it scorches. Amiability is love in its negative form, but when love assumes its positive form, when it becomes an earnest and broad humanity, then it begins to sparkle and flash and smite. *He who reveres the good and cleaves to it, necessarily abhors the evil, and denounces it*; and he who has small abhorrence of evil has usually but a feeble allegiance to good. It was out of the bosom of his loving kindness that Jesus launched the frightful bolts of his invective at the scribes and Pharisees of his time ; clearing the atmosphere of their hypocrisy by dreadful process of thunder-storm, that the common people might not suffocate. *It is out of his heart of infinite pity for the world that the Almighty Father makes the wicked consume away*, and buries faithless nations in shameless graves. He who speaks in the interest of principles cannot be silenced by a refutation ; and he who labors in the cause of man must use the vices of men as his tools.

What seems cruelty to the individual may be mercy to the whole, and to them likewise in the end."* This is well said, though Mr. Parker's denunciations of evil were often tinged with bitterness. But God's threatenings against evil-doers have no taint of bitterness. These are never vindictive. They proceed from a heart of infinite pity, the heart of " the Almighty *Father*."

Now to threaten evil in so many forms, and with such awful emphasis of language, but with no thought of inflicting it, cannot be reconciled with the truth or the benevolence of God. To inflict undeserved evil upon a moral being, without his consent in the way of self-sacrifice, and when no moral benefit is to be derived from it, is injustice and cruelty. And it is as really unjust to threaten such a being with evils which he does not deserve, and to keep him in terror of such acts of cruelty, as to inflict upon him needless and undeserved pain. If we are to hold to the divine benevolence, we must find some fact in man's condition which calls for this infliction of evil from God; and this is

* Rev. O. B. Frothingham.

given in the fact of sin. *Hell is the logical exponent of sin.* Death is the wages of sin.

"*Wages*,"—that which is earned, which is due to him who receives it;—the word meant originally the rations dealt out to soldiers as their pay. It is here set in contrast with the *gift* of God—that eternal life of blessedness which none of our sinful race can deserve, but which is a gratuity bestowed in consequence of what Christ has done. The Life is a gift of grace, not a debt; but the Death is the wages of sin—that which is due to it under the government of God.

What then is the death here threatened? Mere physical death? But all men suffer that, the righteous and the wicked; and the text makes a contrast between death and life as the results of two opposite courses or states of character. As life in the Scriptures is often a synonym for happiness, so death is a synonym for misery. "Life" denotes the highest good which God can bestow upon his creatures; and "Death," the opposite of this, denotes the privation of all good, and the highest misery which God can inflict. "I have set before you life and death, blessing and cursing;"*—blessing is here the equivalent of life, and the curse of God, implying the privation of all good and the infliction of all evil, is the equivalent of death. "In the way of righteousness is life; in the pathway thereof there is no death."† Now the righteous man suffers physical death;—this does lie in his pathway—but the misery which "Death" denotes, he avoids. "Thou wilt show me the path of life; in thy presence is fulness of joy; at thy right hand there are pleasures forevermore."‡—Fulness of joy, pleasures forever, are the equivalent of "life;" and the opposite of this, banishment from God in hopeless misery, is death. "Thou hast made known to me the way of life; thou shalt make me full of joy with thy countenance."‖ The one phrase is the equivalent of the other; the way of life is fulness of joy in the presence of God; and the opposite condition is death. The conviction of

* Deut. xxx: 19. † Prov. xii: 28. ‡ Ps. xvi: 11. ‖ Acts ii: 28.

sin and the consequent misery which the law produces in the soul, is described by Paul as "death."* So "the ministration of condemnation," the law given at Sinai with its penal sanctions, is said to have been "a ministration of death."† Paul says of preachers of the Gospel, "We are unto God a sweet savour of Christ, in them that are saved, and in them that perish. To the one we are the savour of death unto death, and to the other of life unto life."‡ To those who accept the Gospel and are saved, it brings that peace and joy which are life; to those who reject it and perish, it brings that misery which is death. "We know that we have passed from death unto life because we love the brethren."‖ This cannot mean that he who loves his brother will be exempt from physical death; but he is freed from the condemnation and misery of selfishness, which is death. And with a fearful emphasis of wo, the misery that shall come upon the wicked

---

* Romans, Chap vii. and viii. † 2 Cor. 3 : 7.
‡ 2 Cor. 2 : 16. ‖ 1 John 3 : 14.

after physical death, after the resurrection, after the judgment, is called "the second death."* This is the death which is "the wages of sin,"—the equivalent of that dread sentence of the Lord Jesus, " These shall go away into everlasting punishment."

That physical death was in the world before the fall of man, the record of geology clearly teaches. That the human race would in some way have been transferred from this world to other spheres, even had there been no transgression, is highly probable from the law of increase upon the earth itself, and from the law of progress in the moral universe. In what sense, then, was death threatened to Adam as the penalty of sin? " By one man sin entered into the world, and death by sin; and so death passed upon all men, for that all have sinned."* The pain, the grief, the fear, the agony of mortal dissolution, make physical death a standing expression of God's displeasure at sin. But is this all that death implies? The believer in Christ is delivered

---

* Rev. xx : 14.   † Rom. v : 12.

from the fear of death, but not from the physical process of dying, with its attendant suffering. But "the righteous hath *hope* in his death." Hope of what? Hope of some good after the dissolution of the body, which the wicked shall not enjoy—for "the wicked is driven away in his wickedness." That good is denominated "life," while the evil that shall overtake the wicked is described as "death" in continuity. Hence the Scriptures use the term life to denote the normal activity of the soul toward God, and as a synonym of blessedness; and the term death to denote the perversion of the soul from God and goodness, and as a synonym of misery. "Men are represented as *now* dead—dead in sin, dead to God and righteousness—and, as such, under his wrath and curse. And this present death has for its sequel the second death. Both are, to those who remain out of Christ, indivisible parts of one terrible whole. In like manner the converted sinner's *life* begins *in this world* the very day when he is, through repentance and faith, united to

Christ; and it is completed at the resurrection. He has *now* in his soul the dawn of eternal life; and the dawn not only ushers in the day, but is itself a part of it. . . . . . . He that believeth on me, though he die, shall live. And every one that liveth, and believeth on me, shall not die forever."*

To Adam, as yet without experience of pain or suffering, and with no example of death in a human subject, the warning "In the day that thou eatest thereof thou shalt surely die,"† must have suggested the loss of all known or possible good. All this was involved in that original penalty of which the one word Death was the fearful exponent. But the progressive revelation of the realities of the future state unfolded more of the import of that original sentence. To borrow the illustration of another,‡ the sentence of banishment to Siberia, when first pronounced by the Russian Court, signified to its victim

---
* Prof. E. P. Barrow's Bib. Sac., Vol. XV., pp. 641-3.
† Gen. ii : 17.
‡ Rev. N. W. Taylor, D. D.

the loss of home, property, society, and a dreary existence in an unknown region. By and by as reports came back from the exiles, it was understood that Siberia is a region of cold and desolation; that there are dismal mines in which the exiles are worked in chain-gangs; that escape is impossible, return hopeless; and thus the sentence of exile grew to that gigantic terror that the name Siberia now suggests. But all this was known to the government at the first, and was included in the original sentence of banishment to Siberia. So the sentence of death pronounced as the penalty of sin, beginning in the visible loss of the present life and all earthly good, included from the first all those accumulated terrors, which in the parable of Dives, the judgment scene described by Christ, the warnings of Peter, Paul and Jude, and the fearful imagery of the Revelation by John, gather about "the second death."

This death we are told is the wages of Sin, its just desert. And what is sin, that it should deserve such a penalty? "Sin is the transgression of the law;"* sin is wilful rebellion against the known authority of God. And what is that law, the transgression of which demands the penalty of death? Here lies the gist of the whole question. John Quincy Adams is reported to have said that "it is impossible for a man to commit sin enough in this life to deserve eternal damnation." And that remark, I think, contains the pith of the so-called Rationalistic opposition to the doctrine of eternal punishment. Mr. Adams made it a question of How *much* sin? The Bible makes it a question of *the kind of action* that sin is, the character that it denotes, the judgment that it deserves.

—The wages of sin is death.—

Now, the demerit of sin must be determined from the nature and value of the law which it violates. A city ordinance forbids that I should throw ashes into the street. But if I should do this every day of the year,

---

* 1 John iii : 4.

nobody would feel that I deserved to be sent to states-prison or the gallows for such an offence, however much repeated. It would prove me to be a disagreeable neighbor, an obstinate citizen, and I ought to suffer such fines and penalties as are proportioned to the nature of the offence. But not even the daily repetition of such an offence would warrant the taking away of my life or liberty by the law.

But suppose that I should deliberately and wilfully take the life of a fellow man. Could it be urged in mitigation of the penalty which the law annexes to the crime of murder, that this was my *first* offence against human life? When a professor of science in one of our first Universities, murdered a prominent citizen of Boston, did it count in his favor with the jury that this was the first murder with which he was charged; that he was a gentleman of culture, moving in the best circles, accustomed to scholarly society and pursuits, and not addicted to stabbing and shooting men upon the streets? How *many* offences of that sort must one commit, to deserve the highest penalty of the law? Human laws do not graduate their penalties by the number of offences but by the nature of the offence. We all recognize it as a true principle that the value of the law, and the nature of the authority, oppugned by the act of transgression, determine the demerit of the transgressor. A crime against the most sacred trust committed to society, that of human life, or a crime against the very organization and life of society itself,—these two crimes of murder and treason demand the highest form of penalty, because they strike at the most vital point in human law and authority. Our measure of the desert of crime is not mathematical but moral; not given so many offences, to determine how much punishment; but what is the value of the law which is broken and the authority which is rejected?—what interests of society and government are endangered or set at nought?—and what penalty shall be the appropriate expression of this before the community?

Upon this—the only just and sound principle—what is the desert of sin? Sin is the transgression of the law. And what is the law of God? Is it a mere system of police regulations for preserving external order in his moral kingdom, or is it a principle vital to the welfare of that kingdom, set forth by divine authority, so that the violation of this law is a deadly blow aimed at the happiness of the moral universe, and treason against the wisest and best government?

The definition which Blackstone gives of law in general as established among men, may be transferred with much higher significance to the law of God. "Law," he says, "is a rule of civil conduct prescribed by the supreme power in a State, commanding what is right and prohibiting what is wrong." It is a *rule*—as "something permanent, uniform, and universal." Not *advice*, "which we are at liberty to follow or not, as we see proper; for our obedience to the law depends not upon *our approbation*, but upon the *maker's will*." Not "a *compact*"—for "a compact is a promise proceeding *from* us; law is a command directed *to* us. The language of a compact is, I will, or will not, do this; that of a law is, thou shalt, or shalt not do it." It is a rule of conduct prescribed, announced, notified. It is "prescribed by the supreme power," wherever that is vested in the State. It commands what is right and forbids what is wrong; the great object of all true law being to secure right action and to deter men from wrong action.

Take now this clear and admirable definition of law, and by change of terms apply it to the moral law of God. That law is a rule of moral conduct, prescribed by the supreme head of the universe, commanding what is right and forbidding what is wrong. And what Blackstone adds concerning human law is even more forcible here: viz. that "of all the parts of a law the most effectual is the *vindicatory*. For it is but lost labor to say, 'do this, or avoid that,' unless we also declare, 'this shall be the consequence of your non-compliance.' The main strength and force of a law consists in the penalty annexed to it."

The law of God proceeds from rightful authority. Without law, without a declared and acknowledged standard and rule of right, there could be no security and no happiness for the intelligent creation. The moral chaos would be worse than the physical when the earth was without form and void. Not ten men could live and act permanently together without some recognized law. Whatever the circumstances of men and whatever their pursuits, whether the Pilgrims on the Mayflower bearing a free gospel to the new world, or the Pike's Peak miners delving the virgin soil for gold,—whether Arctic explorers on some high errand of hope and humanity, or shipwrecked emigrants working the pumps and watching for some friendly sail—wherever men are, they must have *law* in order to the safety of each and the welfare of all. Society, which is itself a necessity of man's existence in this world, demands law as its basis and support. The State is a normal condition of mankind, and the State can exist only by virtue of *law*. And that higher society of moral beings, in their mutual relations as members of one moral kingdom, demands a law which shall hold these beings to the authority of their common head, and their equal obligations to each other.

God alone can give such a law. His perfect knowledge of the beings to be governed, and of all their powers and relations; his boundless wisdom, to choose what is right and good; his immutable integrity, to stand by his own word, and by that which is right and just and true for his moral kingdom; his supreme benevolence, to prefer always that which is best, and to seek ever the highest welfare of the sentient creation; his almighty power to uphold the authority of his law by appropriate sanctions of reward and penalty; these attributes clothe Jehovah with rightful sovereignty over the moral universe. And he has given to that universe a law which is the transcript of his own moral nature— holiness written in letters of love. This law possesses all the qualities or characteristics which should pertain to a perfect moral law; *universality;* it is a law for all moral beings; *impartiality*—it deals equally with all; *immutability*—never shifting its ground nor changing its demands; *unconditional author·ity*—emanating from the supreme head of the universe, the source of all power, and wisdom, and love.

Suppose now that God *could* give a law, obedience to which would secure the highest welfare of his intelligent creatures. Would not *benevolence* lead him to give that law? If this law was adapted to secure the highest happiness of his moral creation, could he be benevolent if he did not prescribe this as the rule of action for his creatures! But such a law God has given—for it is impossible to conceive of a higher state of happiness than would exist if all moral beings would love God with a full and changeless affection, and would love each the other as himself. It is impossible to have a state of perfect happiness among moral beings,—it is impossible to secure their happiness at all,—without such a law. That law is the expression of God's *love* for his moral creation. How then shall he testify his regard for the law, which is the same thing as his valuation of the highest Right and Good? Must he not annex to it a penalty which shall fairly express his sense of the value of the law, and his regard for the highest welfare of his creatures—as suspended upon this law of love? Suppose he should say, "For you to love one another and obey my law is necessary to your highest happiness. I therefore advise you so to act; but if you choose to do otherwise, I will overlook it and make it all right hereafter."—How much love would God thus show for his creatures?

Suppose he should say, "In order that you may be perfectly happy, I *require* you to love me and to love one another. This is necessary to the highest good. But if you choose to be disobedient and selfish, you will come out just as well in the end." What sort of government would that be? What sort of wisdom? What sort of love?

Now selfishness is diametrically opposed to this law of love. Self-seeking renounces the authority of God; selfishness sets itself against love in every form, and against all that happiness which love, and love only, is fitted to secure. Can you conceive of a worse thing? Is there a worse thing in the universe of God? Is anything wanting but the prevalence of such a spirit, to destroy all good? If even now, under all the restraints of God's law and its threatened penalty, selfishness has brought upon man such a heritage of wo, what misery would it accomplish if those restraints were removed!

Look at it as toward God. Conceive of God in his own being—the most glorious object possible to human thought—his attributes infinite in their perfection, perfect in their infinity. Is he not a God to be admired and praised? Think of God in his character —holiness, goodness, justice, truth, all that can constitute perfection in a moral being, and this too—infinite. Think of God in his works and ways,—his wisdom and beneficence, the order, and beauty, and majesty of his kingdom;—and tell me whether a creature should not give him unbounded homage and affection? And yet this creature man, who has received the magnificent endowment of *will*, lifts up his head and says, "*not thy* will—but MINE." Can wickedness go to a higher reach of daring? Must not a righteous God testify his displeasure at so great a crime? "It is not that God burns with resentment at the affront put upon him; not that he lays aside for a moment any of the goodness of his nature; not as some choose wickedly to pervert things and say that according to Scripture, he brought some of his creatures into existence in order to make them miserable; but his very regard to the universal happiness compels him to maintain his holy law inviolate. Nor can any reasonable person regret that the law of God when violated, should bring suffering to the transgressor, any more than he can regret that fire should burn and water drown those who choose to brave them.—It is not wrath, it is not fury, it is not passion, which lifts the arm of justice against the violater of law, but wisdom and goodness; which is not that blind, indiscriminate easy goodness which some choose to ascribe to God, and which would be a weakness exposing to contempt, rather than a virtue commanding our respect;—but an enlarged and all-comprehending regard to the interests of the whole, with which the well being of the incorrigible transgressor, (if it were possible indeed, which in the nature of things it is not, for a determined despiser of such a law to be happy) could not be allowed to come into competition or bring into jeopardy. So that the very benevolence of God, his considerable regard to the welfare of the many will nerve his arm to inflict the necessary punishment on the rebellious."[*]

Look at this spirit as toward *man* and all the intelligent creation. Not Plato in his ideal republic, nor Sir Thomas More in his

[*] Bellamy.

Utopia; nor Coleridge, Southey, and Wordsworth in their early dream of a pure and equal society—a "pantocracy" to be founded in the choicest Arcadia of nature; nor Fourier in his theory of a community of equality and fraternity; ever rose to such a conception as would be realized by this simple principle, that each should love his neighbor *as himself*—or in the golden rule; "All things whatsoever ye would that men should do to you, do ye even so to them." Selfishness would snap asunder that chain of gold— would put the *I*, the petty interest of one, against the whole community, the whole world, the whole intelligent universe. And this is SIN. Do you call it a light thing and say a man cannot commit sin enough to deserve eternal punishment? Suppose a man pulls up but one rail from a track just before the express train is due, and then goes and takes his position to see the crash. Is not he enough of a villain to be hung, because he didn't tear up the whole track? Selfishness never fully exhibits itself in any single character in life; it acts itself out according to particular inclinations or in opposition to restraints that happen to be felt. But that which it does, shows what it is, and of what it is capable. How then should God act toward sin? Shall he pass it over without censure, without penalty? *Would He be a good being, if he did not hate the worst thing?*—if he did not show displeasure at that which aims to destroy the happiness of his whole creation?

A human governor gives a wise, good, and necessary law. But when it is broken, he says to the transgressors, "Go your way, I shall not harm you." How much does he care for the law? The constitution of California declares that no person who engages in a duel shall hold office. The Chief Justice, sworn to uphold the Constitution, lies in wait for her Senator and challenges him to the bloody field. How much is that law worth? How much is such a Judge worth as a supporter of law? Or if he do not himself violate law, suppose he remits the penalty at will to the transgressor. How much is law worth in such hands? Suppose he says, in excuse for this wicked and dangerous leniency, that the transgressors are his *children!* The holy angels look down upon a sinning world, they see its frightful crimes, its cruelties, and woes; and are told that these are only the freaks and sports of God's children, which He does not feel called upon to punish!

Suppose that God should manifest toward sin *less* displeasure than He is capable of feeling? By what standard would you then measure his holiness and his love? Is not the principle already quoted strictly true, that "he who has small abhorrence of evil has but a feeble allegiance to good?" God as a perfect moral governor, must prefer *holiness* to all things else, as essential to the highest happiness of his creatures, and must show his highest approbation of obedience and highest disapprobation of disobedience. Will any pretend that this expression is made in the present life? The evils here inflicted are indeed a testimony against sin. But they fall unevenly—not always the most evil to the most wicked; they are modified by tokens of favor and mercy; and never do we see that degree of evil which could be taken as God's full expression of his displeasure at sin. These evils warn us of what is possible in that direction. The Psalmist was perplexed at the prosperity of the wicked, as arguing God's indifference to sin;—"until I went into the sanctuary of God; then understood I *their end*. Surely thou didst set them in slippery places; thou castedst them down into destruction."* God must put forth his express condemnation of sin, in the way of penalty, as the sanction of his moral government. Must there not be a future retribution? Could we be satisfied of the holiness and love of God, if the world should wind up just as it is, and there be no discriminating judgment, and no retribution in the hereafter?

1. *The punishment which God threatens*

* Ps. lxxiii : 17, 18.

against the wicked is dictated not by vindictive feeling, but by supreme benevolence. The moral character of God is one pure central flame of love—a light that we could not look upon, and live. But this light is ensphered as it were in crystal of many hues, and this revolves upon us the various attributes of God. Where shines the crystal-white, his holiness beams forth upon us from that central fount of love. With softened tone his goodness and mercy are diffused from that same living flame. But ever and anon the red flame of justice flashes out upon us from the same inward source; not vindictive vengeance, but love guarding his holy law. And because God is a being of perfect love, there is no hope for an incorrigible sinner. God has shown his utmost love for men in the gift of his Son to die for them; but by that same gift he has shown his love for his law; and he demands that men shall honor that law by confession and repentance, and shall honor that Son by faith and love. If they will not honor both the law and the Son, how can God honor either by saving them?

That everlasting life which is the highest felicity of the soul, is the fruition of a life of holiness here begun. It is " the *gift* of God through Jesus Christ," and thus stands contrasted with that death which is the just due of sin. The life is to be obtained only upon the terms on which it is proffered—repentance and faith in the Lord Jesus Christ, and a new life bringing forth fruit unto holiness. If these terms of deliverance which Divine Love now proffers at so great a cost to itself, be not accepted, then truth, and equity, and love demand that the law shall take its inexorable course, and that sin which has outraged all goodness and mercy, shall receive the fit recompense of death.

2. *The deeper our insight into the evil of sin, the stronger our conviction of the doctrine of future retribution.* The holiest minds have commonly had the liveliest apprehension of the reality of hell; not as a morbid fear on their part—for " there is no condemnation to

them that are in Christ ;" nor with a self complacent indifference to the fate of others, since they themselves were secure in Christ; but because they have measured the deeps of sin in their own hearts; because they have learned something of the majesty of holiness in God. It is upon this principle that the Bible represents all Heaven as acquiescent in the final doom of the wicked. "Salvation, and glory, and honor, and power, unto the Lord our God; for true and righteous are his judgments."*

The nature and demerit of sin is the turning point of this whole discussion. If sin is itself a vitiated physical nature fastened upon men by birth and inheritance; if sin is merely the offspring of ignorance or the incidental result of circumstances; if sin is organic and not personal, residing not in the individual will but in the constitution of society; in a word, if sin is the product of any efficient cause whatever outside of the free individual choice of the sinner; then it not only cannot

* Rev. xix : 1, 2.

deserve eternal punishment, but it cannot deserve punishment at all.* But individual consciousness, and the history of human society and legislation, forbid any such view of sin. When we contemplate sin as it is, in relation to the law of love and in its bearing upon the government of God and the welfare of the moral universe, then we see how holy, and just and good is that decree, "The wages of sin is death."

3. *Sinners who shall perish hereafter will have none to blame but themselves.* Sin, SIN will have ruined them. And what is sin but their own act? Can we charge that upon God? All men know better. If God made men sin, conscience would never upbraid. You ask why he made you capable of sinning. And would you have him annihilate the glorious endowment of moral freedom with its immeasurable capacity for good, just because you have abused that freedom for evil? Ah, not nature, nor providence, nor law, but *sin*

---

* This thought is expanded in the succeeding lecture.

and sin only will be your ruin. And in the deepest cavern of despair, there is no sound so appalling as that cry of self-condemnation and self-ruin, "*The wages of sin is death.*"

LECTURE V.

No Future Probation Revealed or Probable.

Luke xvi : 22. *Seq.* [*The parable of Dives and Lazarus.*]

The latest refuge of Universalism is in the doctrine of the *final restoration* of all men to virtue and happiness. Few of the advocates of that system will now avow the bolder forms of statement in which the doctrine was once put forth; that all the evil consequences of sin are suffered in the present life, and that death will bring to all men alike immunity from suffering, and the enjoyment of pure and endless felicity in heaven. Men of intelligence, and of sound moral and philanthropic sentiments, can hardly fail to see that to affirm that judgment and hell are bugbears, and that there will be hereafter no retribution for sin, and no difference of condition between the righteous and the wicked, is to remove from the passions of men all the restraints of God's moral government, and to reduce that government to the caricature of a law without sanctions and an authority without support. Such men, while disowning a doctrine so contrary to reason and Scripture, and so hurtful to morality, if they would maintain at all the doctrine of universal salvation, must do this under some form of *restoration;* either a renewed probation after death; or a purgatorial discipline for sin; or a satisfaction in equity to the divine law by a measure of punishment answerable to the offense; or a universal amnesty to be hereafter proclaimed by Jehovah to all rebels against his authority. This doctrine of restoration is now the strong point of the advocates of universal salvation, as distinguished from believers in the doctrine of the annihilation of the wicked;—it is the type of the respectable and fashionable Universalism of our time. The leading organs and advocates of that system of faith distinctly avow their belief that God administers a moral government with legal sanctions to be dispensed through happiness and misery hereafter; that there will be after death, a discriminating judgment upon character, and a retribution of evil for iniquity; but they deny that this evil will be unmitigated and eternal. Indeed some writers have argued that the principles of God's moral government, while requiring that sin should be punished, yet limit that punishment in degree and duration. It may prove, however, that in thus attempting to seize upon the armory of divine retribution for their own defense, they have but shut themselves up in a prison whence the combined forces of reason and scripture will dislodge them, turning even their chosen arguments against themselves.

The parable of Dives and Lazarus describes men in two opposite conditions after death. The whole point and force of the parable lies in the contrast which it sets up between the respective conditions of the beggar and the rich man here and hereafter. While the rich man was clothed in purple and fine linen, and fared sumptuously every day, the beggar lay at his gate, full of sores, desiring to be fed with the crumbs which fell from his table. This is the first contrast—a contrast of condition not directly connected with character :—the contrast of a pious beggar with a luxurious worldling. Both now suffer the common lot of men, and pass from this world into another state of being. The beggar died, and so poor was he that, even if he had a decent burial, the fact was not worth mentioning ;—but he was carried into Abraham's bosom ; he went from his poverty and suffering to share the felicity of Abraham in heaven. No one can question that this describes a state of happiness after death.

The rich man also died, and was buried with whatever of pomp and circumstance pertained to his position ; "and in hell he lifted up his eyes being in torments." This, then, was his condition after death. Like Lazarus he passed into another state of being; he was not annihilated but continued to exist; he retained his personal identity, his consciousness, and his memory; but he did not go to heaven; he went to a place afar off from Abraham and Lazarus; to a place of torments, of positive and conscious suffering; a place from which he saw no possibility of deliverance, and in which he found no means of relief. Who can doubt that there is prepared for the ungodly after death a place of positive suffering? Whether we take the objective or the subjective interpretation of the parable, whether we understand it to describe pain inflicted by external causes, or mental anguish, if we admit that Christ knew anything of the future, and that he accurately described it, we must admit that there will be hereafter for the wicked, a state of conscious, positive, unmitigated suffering—a suffering like that of one consumed with raging fever, yet unable to gain the poor relief of a drop of water to the tongue.

But, moreover, the parable sheds a fearful light upon the duration of this state of misery. When Dives cries only for momentary relief, Abraham answers, "Between us and you there is a great gulf fixed;" a *gulf* of separation; a *great* gulf, yawning, deep; a *fixed* gulf, unchangeable, impassable, "so that they which would pass from hence to you cannot, neither can they pass to us that would come from thence;" no crossing from heaven with relief, no crossing to escape from hell: a deep, yawning chasm that no plummet of hope can sound, that no skill or desperation can bridge over; a great gulf fixed between heaven and hell. Do you say this is figurative, poetic language? Our Lord has declared the same thing in these emphatic words: "These shall go away into everlasting punishment."

But look at another point. Dives who does not so much as ask a renewed probation for himself, or anticipate deliverance through repentance and expiatory suffering, begs not that *he* may be released from hell to warn men of that place of torment, but that Lazarus may go back to earth upon that mission;

and is answered that all needed means of instruction and grace have been provided for men, and "if they will not hear Moses and the prophets, neither will they be persuaded though one rose from the dead." The provisions of mercy in this world of probation are so rich and full that none need hope for other terms and agencies. But if no addition will be made to the means now used to deter men from going to hell, is there any reasonable ground to expect that other means will or can be used hereafter to deliver those who shall have fallen into perdition?

I may sum up the statement upon this point in the form of the seventh proposition laid down in my introductory discourse.

VII. *Since the desert of punishment to the sinner arises from that endowment of free agency which is essential to the attainment of that peculiar blessedness which is only within the reach of a moral being: and since the means of recovery from sin, and of deliverance from condemnation can be made available only in the use of that same free agency of the sinner; and since the love of God has made the most ample provision of pardon, and has proffered this to the sinner with divine compassion and importunity,—but only in vain: there remains no conceivable mode, as there is no revealed promise, by which the Fatherhood of God can make one dying in impenitence and unbelief, holy and blessed in the future world.*

Two or three propositions embodied in this, require to be considered in their order, as having a direct bearing upon the main question—Whether there will be a renewed probation, or any mode of restoration for the wicked after death.

1. *Desert of punishment arises from the free agency of the sinner in his transgression.*

If God were in any wise responsible for the sinner's act of disobedience to his own law; if He had the least causative agency in the act of transgression, then it would not only be monstrous to punish the sinner *eternally*, —it would be despotic and cruel to punish him at all.—If sin were the necessary result of circumstances, an incident or accident of society, government, education, law, then it would not only be cruel to punish the sinner eternally, but unjust and cruel to punish him for a single moment

Wherever there is sin there is a *sinner*, in whose personality centers the responsibility of the act. The social revel, the wine dinner, the saloon, the dram-shop, example, custom, temptations, may lead a man to indulge himself in liquor till he becomes a drunkard; but after all, if he becomes a drunkard it is because *he drinks*, knowing the peril to which this exposes him—drinks when he has power to refrain from drinking, and so makes himself a drunkard. Hence, however censurable the customs of society, however mischievous the laws that tolerate and shield the agencies of intemperance, however wicked the tempters, the *sin* of drunkenness lies at his own door. It is sometimes argued that the sins of men are mere foibles or mistakes, resulting from ignorance, weakness, social influence, defective physical organization and the like, and that therefore it is incredible that a just and good God should punish sinners eternally. But if any of these things is an efficient cause of the act of transgression, then there is no culpability in that act, and it would be unjust to punish the transgressor at all. If social organization, physical temperament, cerebral structure, or anything but moral choice is the efficient cause of sin, then sin no more deserves punishment than does physical deformity or scarlet fever.

But what is sin? It is " the voluntary departure of a moral agent from the known rule of rectitude or duty, prescribed by God ;" or in the briefer phrase of Scripture, it is " the transgression of the law." There can be no sin where there is not in the offender the full power of contrary choice. "Let no man say when he is tempted, I am tempted of God: for God cannot be tempted with evil, neither tempteth he any man. But every man is tempted when he is drawn away of his own lust,"—his constitutional desires which ought to be under the guidance of reason, his yearnings after natural good, which ought to be directed and controlled by conscience and the rule of right,—"every man is tempted when he is drawn away of his own carnal appetite and enticed; then when lust hath conceived, it bringeth forth sin; and sin when it is finished bringeth forth death."* The sin begins in the voluntary act of indulging mere natural desires beyond or against the restraints of the known law of God written in reason, conscience, and the Bible.

Whatever psychological theory we may adopt as to the manner in which a free agent capable of knowing and doing right yields himself to do wrong, *consciousness* testifies that he does act freely in the wrong he does, and in this voluntariness lies the sinfulness of the act. The nature of this act was considered in the last discourse. It was shown that God's law is love, and is essential to the well-being of the whole moral creation; and therefore that the transgression of this law,

* Jas i : 14, 15.

both in the spirit and in the scope of the act, is the most deadly crime against the authority of God and the happiness of the universe of which we can conceive; an act requiring from Him as a just and benevolent ruler the highest possible expression of his displeasure. The act of treason against the law of love, cannot be too much abhorred, too sorely condemned, by the God of love.

But that act implies an actor with a personal responsibility. The desert of punishment for sin grows out of complete free agency in the act of sinning. Do you say then that this free agency is the gift of God? Most assuredly it is; and one of the noblest, best of gifts. It is the crowning perfection of man as a creature; it is an essential condition of happiness for a moral being;— "self-knowing, and from thence magnanimous to correspond with heaven." It is this that makes you capable of love, capable of holiness, capable of the boundless purity and bliss of heaven: and because you so pervert this sublime gift of God, your sin hath the greater condemnation.

The spiritual kingdom of God can be established only in intelligent minds, and it can be established in such minds only with their free consent. It matters not that the omnipotence of Jehovah could protect his throne from external violence ; it matters not that he could impose upon rebellious creatures physical restraints that would make them powerless for evil ;—whenever an intelligent being freely transgresses the law of God and refuses to render homage to Jehovah, the kingdom of God is annulled within that soul. It matters not that the occasion or the outward expression of such disobedience is in itself trivial—the moral act is stupendous. When Adam took of the forbidden fruit he set up a conflict of jurisdiction, of supremacy, between his Maker and himself. That freedom of will which exalted him above all other creatures upon earth as the image of God, was put forth in direct hostility to the positive and known will of the Creator.

2. *Our proposition affirms that the means of recovery from sin and of deliverance from condemnation can be made available only in the use of this same free agency of the sinner.*

Most advocates of universal salvation admit that there is some demerit in sin, something blameable or punishable in the moral conduct of men from which they need deliverance; but they claim that this deliverance is, or will be, accomplished for all men through the death of Christ. The mere Deist may not admit that there is such a thing as sin in the sense just now defined— free moral action against the known law of God, and deserving its penalty. A personal friend of Mr. Theodore Parker* has lately said of him in his own pulpit, "I must frankly say that I think Theodore Parker has not had any experience of sin in this kind. In him sin is either ignorance of God's law, which he pities and would enlighten; weakness, which he pities, and would help; or wilfulness, which he hates and rebukes." One

---

* Rev. James Freeman Clarke.

whose views of sin are so narrow and imperfect, cannot feel the need of a great salvation. "Reform and cure yourself," would be his motto. But the very term salvation implies deliverance from actual peril, and if there is any significance in the phrase universal salvation there must be some universal peril to be escaped. The concession of many who hold that belief is, that men are sinful and condemned, but that sooner or later, in one way or another, the redemption of Christ will prove effectual for the entire human race. Now the point upon which I would here fix attention is, that the deliverance of any sinner from that guilt and condemnation into which his free agency has plunged him by transgression, can be effected only in the use of that same free agency in accepting the terms of deliverance. God has provided *a* salvation from sin, a way of escape from condemnation. This salvation is adequate for all, this way of escape is open to all. The atonement of Christ as a provision of divine love, magnifying the law in vouchsafing pardon, is all that the whole race of man in all its generations can need as a provision for salvation. But what then? The atonement of Christ while vindicating and sustaining the law, brings all the potency of divine love to persuade the sinner to turn to God, and invites him to trust in Christ with a cordial, self-renouncing, self-consecrating faith. *Can* there be any deliverance from the sinful state of the soul itself, until the choice of the sinner shall be transferred from the world and self to God? His sin lies in the will, and his holiness must begin there, or there is no possible salvation from sin. This lies in the very nature of the mind.

Or is there any promise of deliverance from condemnation, except through an intelligent cordial faith in Christ as the Redeemer? "He that believeth on him is not condemned; but he that believeth not is condemned already, because he hath not believed in the name of the only begotten Son of God."*—Faith is the sealing act that

---

* John iii: 18.

ensures personal salvation under the general and free provision for salvation by the atonement. The atonement of Christ, therefore, argues nothing, proves nothing for the actual salvation of any individual sinner. It proves only the willingness and the desire of God to pardon whosoever will repent and believe. But how many die impenitent and unbelieving. And if the atonement should be ten times repeated in the future state, this would avail nothing without the personal repentance and faith of the condemned. But we have no evidence that it will be repeated, and none that the stubborn will which has refused it here would ever accept it there.

3. We must note that *God has made the most ample provision for pardon in this life, through the death of his Son; and has proffered this to the sinner with divine compassion and importunity; and if all this is in vain, there remains no conceivable mode, by which God could hereafter restore to holiness and happiness one dying in impenitence and unbelief.*

Men pass out of the world with characters exceedingly diverse. Will that diversity of character continue in the future without change, with a corresponding diversity of condition also unchanging, or will there be hereafter an opportunity for the wicked to retrieve what they have lost in this life, or by the experience of suffering to become renewed as they never were renewed by the experience of mercy? The study of individual character and of the race in its history, shows that there is a tendency in a depraved character to perpetuate itself, unless wrought upon by some transforming influence from without. No thorough and permanent renovation of character takes place in this life without such influence. Will then any such influence be applied in the future state for the recovery of lost souls to holiness and happiness? Will they to whom the issue of the present state of trial is unfavorable, be favored with another probation beyond the grave?

This question can be answered only from the Scriptures. We can form no opinion on such a point from *a priori* reasoning. There is no analogy in nature, in history, or in Providence, that throws the least light upon it, or even assists us to a conjecture. The fact that this world has been a probation warrants no assumption that there will be such a state hereafter—for the angels that sinned have had *no* probation since their fall. Since a state of probation in the future could exist only through the will of God to exercise further mercy toward those who had rejected mercy in this life, we must reverently inquire what he has made known to us in his own Word, touching his will or purpose upon that point.

If the Scriptures teach us either directly or by fair implication that there will be a state of probation after death, that will determine the question beyond controversy in the affirmative. If the Scriptures teach or fairly imply the contrary, then the question is determined with equal certainty in the negative. It is therefore a matter of inquiry and interpretation as to the teachings of the Scriptures.

Leaving annihilation out of view, there are but three modes conceivable in which the future punishment of those dying in their sins could be brought to an end. These are *first*, that a limited period of suffering should fully expiate their offenses; or *secondly*, that they should be pardoned in view of repentance and reformation induced by suffering; or *thirdly*, that there should be a general amnesty for offenders proclaimed by Jehovah under some new dispensation of clemency.

(1,) But that sinners dying in impenitency should hereafter expiate their offenses by suffering, is impossible both under the terms of the law and the conditions of grace. I have already shown that the nature of sin as the highest conceivable offense against the authority of God, and the highest possible wrong against the welfare of his intelligent creation, demands of Him as a benevolent ruler the strongest possible expression of his displeasure. No limited amount of punishment could make that expression.

Moreover the law of love demands unfaltering obedience at every moment: and the sinner condemned for disobedience in the past, could never make restitution by any obedience or endurance of his own. And still farther, the only ground of admission into heaven for any of our race which the Bible recognizes, is faith in the atoning blood of Christ. But if sinners can expiate their offenses by future punishment, by and by there will be an irruption into heaven from the prison of wo, of those who have served out their time, and who shall enter the heavenly city not with "robes washed in the blood of the Lamb," but with the smell of purgatorial fire upon their garments—who shall go there not as Christians, for they never followed Christ, but rejected Him; not as redeemed, for they never accepted redemption through the sufferings of Christ, but paid the cost of transgression by their own sufferings; and to all eternity these can never join in the song—" To

Him that was slain, and hath redeemed us to God by his blood." Is there anything in the Bible view of heaven that admits the possibility of such an addition to its inmates?

(2.) The second supposition is that the condemned sinners may hereafter be pardoned and restored in view of repentance and reformation induced in them by suffering. But this supposition entirely mistakes the design of punishment. It proceeds upon the notion that the sole design of punishment is the reformation of the offender. Now the reformation of the offender forms no part at all of the design of *legal penalty*. God uses with men in this world admonitory and corrective discipline, for this is a world of probation and not of retribution, and the Bible teaches that judgment and penalty are suspended in order that means of reformation may be tried. The penalty due to sin is not inflicted here. But in the economy of law it is never the part of penalty to reform the offender. The lawmaker does not say to the subject of the law —" Do this and you shall have protection and reward; but if you choose to disobey you shall be punished until you repent and promise to do better." The lawgiver says by word or deed, "This law is required for the welfare of the community; and in order that it shall be respected, I will annex to it a penalty to deter men from breaking it; and will punish transgressors to show that I am in earnest in making such a law, and in the determination to uphold it." The sole design of the penalty *as* penalty is to sustain the law.

"The chief evil of any crime, on account of which it principally deserves punishment, consists in the relaxation of the laws and government of the community in which the crime is committed. For example, the chief evil of theft is not that a certain person is clandestinely deprived of his property. His property may be restored and he may in this respect sustain no damage. Still the thief deserves punishment. If a man be defamed, the chief evil is not that the person defamed is injured by the loss of his reputation. His reputation may, by a full confession of the defamer or by other means, be restored. Still the defamer may deserve punishment. If a man be murdered, the chief evil is not that the man is deprived of his life, and his friends and the community are deprived of the benefit of his aid. His life may have been a burden to himself, to his friends and to the community; or he may by divine power be raised from the dead. Still, in either case, the murderer would deserve punishment.

"The true reason, why all these criminals would, in all these cases deserve punishment is, that by their respective crimes they would weaken the laws and government of the community, thereby would break in upon the public peace, good order, safety and happiness; instead of these would introduce confusion and ruin; and thus would do a very great damage to the community. Therefore they would respectively deserve just so much punishment, as by restoring the tone of the laws and government, would reëstablish the peace, good order, safety and happiness of the community, and thus would repair the damage done to the community by their crimes. A punishment adequate to this end exhibits by the natural evil of it, a just idea of the moral evil of the crime, and a proper motive to restrain all from the commission of it."*

This is the only just and logical view of the infliction of penalty under human law. The penalty is concerned solely in the care of the law; its authority, its sanctity, its majesty. It can admit therefore of no compromise with an offender. I have recently met in a journal which advocates the doctrine of the restoration of the wicked, the following curious statement of belief upon that point: "All the pains and penalties which have been spoken of for ages as an unquenchable fire, are designed not to destroy men, but to save them. They are meant for correction alone, not vengeance. Nor does any other idea of punishment seem Christian in its character, or worthy the Divine attributes. We reject the common theory of eternal tortures, because, confessedly, it is of a purely vindictive char-

---

* President Edwards.

acter, and does not look to the reformation of a single sinner. Punishment which has no higher purpose than the infliction of pain, is nothing but cruelty; and no man ever inflicts it except in moments of great anger; in calmer hours he thinks only of correcting a child's faults."

Of course to inflict pain for the sake of inflicting it, is cruelty. But is there no alternative between mere discipline for reformation and such cruelty? May not a father banish from his house a reckless, debauched, incorrigible son, who is corrupting and destroying the family? May not love for his family require that even with tears and agony he should cut off the child whose reformation seems hopeless? We deny that God's punishments are vindictive; that the element of revenge enters into them at all. They are demanded by that love for his moral creatures which would shield them from the assaults of wickedness.

The same journal says, "In rejecting eternal punishments, we believe in future ones.

The evil consequences of sins are not confined to the precise moment when they are committed, but follow us to another city or the Spirit-world. How long they may trouble us in the Future life no one can estimate. It does not impugn the mercy of God to ascribe any severity or duration to our sufferings, so long as they are designed to reform the soul." But suppose it will not reform? For what is it punished? For having sinned? Or for not having repented? Most true is it that "Law is obligated to punish the transgressor, as much as the transgressor is obligated to obey the law."* We cannot say "God may be just or not as he pleases." He has no choice in the premises. He must be just or he cannot be God.

It is a groundless assumption that suffering works out moral purification by a natural law. Sometimes temporal afflictions lead men to consider their spiritual wants and to seek the good of their higher nature. And when once the heart has been renewed by grace and has

* Prof. Shedd

entered into filial relations with God, the discipline of suffering has a tendency to purify its affections from earthly dross, and to bring it into a fuller participation of the divine holiness. But this is not strictly the tendency of suffering as such, but of that gracious disposition which leads the humble and believing soul to use suffering for its own profit. How often, alas, does suffering not only fail to purify the soul from sin, but aggravate and intensify its selfish and malignant passions, and make it a very fiend.

Mœhler argues that those who leave this world still bearing about them stains of sin, must pass through a place of purification before entering heaven.* But this doctrine of a spiritual purification by purgatory does not take into account the real enormity of sin as the voluntary transgression, by an intelligent being, of the known will of God; but proceeds upon the old pagan philosophy that sin is a physical contamination resident in the

* Symbolism.

flesh, which may be exterminated like a cancer, by the knife and the fire.

Beside, if purgatory is a necessary prelude to heaven for sinful souls, why pray that men should be delivered from it? Moreover, this notion of a purgatorial purification changes the whole basis of salvation under the Gospel, from grace through Christ, to desert through obedience rendered and penalty endured. When a soul emerges from this purgatory into heaven, how can it praise Christ for a purification which it has wrought out through its own sufferings? And farther; to assume that because suffering in this world is sometimes made a means of discipline and purification, and is not always penal evil, therefore it will be disciplinary and not penal hereafter, is to beg the whole question.

(3.) The only remaining supposition is that God will in some way interpose by special clemency hereafter, to release the wicked. But upon what is such an expectation grounded? God was under no obligation to provide the means of pardon which he has provided in the present life. He has made no such provision for the fallen angels. But if his benevolence requires that he should give wicked men a *second* trial of his grace, why does it not equally require at least one offer of pardon to *devils?* God has nowhere promised or intimated any such act of grace in the future as possible. On the contrary, he has threatened just the opposite. But the omniscient God already knows all that he purposes to do in the future; and if He really intends to release the condemned by an act of clemency, why does He, with all the solemnity of his word, threaten them with everlasting punishment? Is this honest? Is it true? Could you rely upon the word of such a Being in anything? Either he must change his mind without any change of outward facts—or he says he will do what he has no thought of doing.

As to grace in the future—what can God do more than He has already done in the gift of his Son, and by the urgency of his Spirit, to bring sinners to repentance? Are not the tender mercies of Jehovah concentrated in the cross? To those who humbly, gratefully accept the grace of God in Christ, the cross is the pledge of all future good. "He that spared not his own son, but delivered him up for us all, how shall he not also with him freely give us all things."* But to those who despise and reject the grace of God in Christ, the cross itself becomes the argument and the warning of a more fearful retribution. "Of how much sorer punishment shall he be thought worthy, who hath trodden under foot the Son of God?"†

Since God has already granted a probation of grace to sinners condemned by law, since he has given the ample warnings and entreaties of his Word, since he has given his own Son to humiliation and agony and death that he might save lost men, since he has sent his Holy Spirit to move upon them and reclaim them, since he has waited with much long-suffering to win men to repentance here, and they knowing that this was their probation,

---

* Rom. viii: 32.   † Heb. x : 29.

have resisted all these influences, and hardened their hearts in impenitency, can there be even a shadow of a plea that goodness will grant them another probation?

The Bible everywhere assumes that present means of grace are adequate and will be final. Christ makes the condemnation and final rejection of the wicked hinge upon their rejection of the Gospel in the present life. " God so loved the world that he gave his only begotten son that whosoever believeth in him should not perish, but have everlasting life."* The alternative of perishing or having life turns upon each one's treatment of Christ as he is *now* presented in the Gospel. This alternative meets us upon almost every page of the New Testament. " He that believeth on Him is not condemned, but he that believeth not is condemned already because he, hath not believed in the name of the only begotten Son of God."*

Again, the duty of accepting Christ in this life is presented with an urgency and a fre-

* John iii : 16 † John iii : 16.

quency that compel the belief that this is man's only probation. "Seek ye the Lord while he may be found; call ye upon him while he is near.*" "Now is the accepted time; now is the day of salvation."† "How shall we escape if we neglect so great salvation?"‡ The shortness of time, the nearness of death, the approach of the judgment, are urged continually in the Bible as motives to immediate repentance. Death is represented as making a great change for eternity. It is the closing up of probation. "Whatsoever thy hand findeth to do, do it with thy might; for there is no work, nor device, nor knowledge, nor wisdom, in the grave, whither thou goest."§ The Bible represents this as the only dispensation of grace; in which all possible measures of recovery are exhausted. "If we sin wilfully after that we have received the knowledge of the truth, there remaineth no more sacrifice for sins, but a certain fearful looking for of judgment and

---

* John iii : 18.   † Is. lv : 6.   ‡ Heb. ii : 3.
§ Ecc. ix : 10.

of fiery indignation, that shall devour the adversaries. He that despised Moses' law died without mercy under two or three witnesses; of how much sorer punishment suppose ye shall he be thought worthy who hath trodden under foot the Son of God, and hath counted the blood of the covenant wherewith he was sanctified an unholy thing, and hath done despite unto the Spirit of grace. It is a fearful thing to fall into the hands of the living God."* Men are to be judged hereafter for deeds done "in the *body*."

To recur to the parable of Dives. The rich man is not represented as praying or hoping for deliverance; he does not dream of release from torment; he craves only mitigation; but no messenger of mercy can go to him. Then he prays that a messenger from the unseen world may go to his five brethren yet on earth, and warn them against the place of torment. The answer teaches the sufficiency of the present means of grace, and that nothing will be added thereto. Men must be-

* Heb. x : 26—31.

lieve the Bible as they have it; not look for spirits to certify it from the unseen world. No further revelation will be given; no higher means employed; therefore believe and act under *present* responsibility, with heaven and hell before you!

And to crown all, in the parable of the virgins, the Saviour represents those who were negligent as coming *after* the probation is over, but the door is shut. They knock and beg, but it opens not; nay, a voice comes from within that silences all hope: "Depart, I know you not."* When death comes, the door of probation, the door of opportunity, the door of salvation is shut; and who shall ever open it again?

At this stage of the discussion the argument from safety—sometimes unduly pressed, sometimes scornfully rejected—is appropriate and urgent. It is wise to *make sure* of eternal salvation in this life, and to *risk* nothing for the future. No advocate of a future pro-

* Matt. xxv: 12.

bation has ever been able to make out from reason even the slightest *probability* of such a state. His moral arguments are mere assumptions. He assumes that the sin of a finite creature is not great enough in the sight of God to call for endless punishment, and therefore he says that God cannot mean this when he threatens it. He assumes that God is too good to punish, and therefore he cannot mean to execute the threatenings of his law. But all this is mere guess-work—nay, it is sheer presumption. What can we know of God's intentions aside from his declarations? And if you bring the theory to the Bible, what do you there find to support it? Not one positive, explicit declaration, that those who die impenitent shall be finally restored and saved; not even that vagueness of statement from which the ingenuity of criticism could torture a conjecture that there *may* be another state of probation; but the whole tenor of the Scriptures, every warning, every call, every entreaty, forbids that supposition. And are you willing to take your chance of a second probation and final recovery on such grounds, and to throw away the certainty of salvation by abusing this probation? Will any man in his senses take that risk? Did Christ mean anything when he asked, "What will it profit if a man gain the whole world and lose his own soul"?* And will you risk the loss of your soul on the meagre conjecture of a future probation? You know this is a state of probation; you know that here you may make sure of eternal life. You know that this probation will end. Then comes death, and after death—*what next?* "It is appointed to man once to die, and after this THE JUDGMENT!"† This you know; but of a second probation you know nothing—nothing from reason, nothing from the Bible, absolutely nothing. And will you risk your soul on such a nothing, when by faith in Christ you can make heaven yours? "Behold, *now* is the accepted time, NOW is the day of salvation." "To-day, if ye will hear his voice, harden not your hearts."

---

* Matt. xvi: 26. † Heb. ix: 27.

LECTURE VI.

The Immortality of the Soul.

Job xiv: 14. *If a man die, shall he live again?*

II Tim. i: 10. *Who hath abolished death, and hath brought life and immortality to light through the Gospel.*

Ten centuries at least intervened between these two utterances touching death and the future state. Both proceeded from devout minds in the near contemplation of death— old men, of large experience, of high religious character, but at the time bereft of all earthly good. Job, a patriarchal prince of wealth, of benevolence, and of integrity, finds himself in a moment stripped of his property and his children, smitten with a painful and loathsome disease, shunned and even mocked by the neighbors he had so long befriended, and tantalized with charges of pride, hypocrisy, and wickedness by the friends who came to condole with him in his afflictions. Overwhelmed with calamity, destitute, afflicted, tormented, clothed with sackcloth, sitting in ashes, forsaken or persecuted by men, his flesh wasted with pain, his soul weary of life, he yet clings to his faith in God, saying, "Though he slay me, yet will I trust him." But the shadow of despondency at times overcast his future. To him the grave was a "land of darkness, and of the shadow of death, without any order." There was no clear and certain light beyond. "There is hope of a tree. if it be cut down, that it will sprout again, and that the tender branch thereof will not cease. Though the root thereof wax old in the earth, and the stock thereof die in the ground, yet through the scent of water it will bud, and bring forth boughs like a plant. But man dieth and wasteth away—or is cut off—yea man giveth up the ghost, and where is he?"* "If a man die, shall he live again?" And the venerable patriarch sitting amid the ruins of his tents, lifts his sunken eyes and searches the broad horizon of the east, but sees there only the faintest twilight disputing the boundary of the night.

Paul also is an old man and has suffered the loss of all things. Though he has not known wealth or family ties, this is because he has voluntarily relinquished the brightest earthly prospects for a despised and hated name. And now he finds himself a prisoner, liable at any moment to be led to execution as a criminal. He has had no wasting disease to weary him of life, but in robust health is to be cut off by a violent death. Friends have forsaken him; and when summoned to court there is no one to stand by him.† But there is no darkness or doubt before him. He writes to his beloved Timothy, "God hath not given us the spirit of fear: but of power, and of love, and of a sound mind. Be not thou therefore ashamed of the testimony of

* Job xiv: 7—11. † II Tim. iv 16.

our Lord, nor of me his prisoner."* But though bound as a victim for the block, his soul is not under bonds of death. Faith unbars his prison ; the extacy of hope casts down his dungeon walls; and beyond the martyr's block he sees Him who by his cross " abolished death, and brought life and immortality to light."

The distinction between Job and Paul in their anticipations of the future, does not lie in different degrees of faith in the wisdom, the justice, and the goodness of God, but in different degrees of knowledge as to the provision made for the righteous in the future. If Paul could say, " I know whom I have believed, and am persuaded that he is able to keep that which I have committed to him against that day ;"† Job could say, with reference either to a resurrection from the dead, or a resuscitation from wasting disease and the vindication of his character over the frailty of the body—" I know that my Redeemer

---

* II Tim. i : 7, 8.   † II Tim. i : 12.

(or Deliverer) liveth, and that at length he will appear upon the earth, and though this body be wasted away, yet in my flesh I shall see God."* But to Paul the resurrection of Jesus was a certified fact; and he trusted not only in the general principles of God's character and government which Job derived from the light of nature or the dawning of revelation, but in the specific mode of redemption and salvation brought to light in the Gospel. The faith of the Apostle was not higher in kind than the faith of the patriarch, but was more definite and complete as to its object, and therefore had greater power to comfort and sustain him. What to Job was a land of the shadow of death, without any order, to Paul was illuminated by the resurrection of Christ, and the higher revelation made to him touching the future condition of the righteous.

Our argument for a future retribution has thus far assumed the continued existence of the soul after death. It is important, however, that we should investigate that fact in

---

* Job xix : 25, 26.

the light of evidence from Nature, from the Hebrew Scriptures, and from the New Testament. I propose, therefore, from these several points of observation, to examine the question of THE IMMORTALITY OF THE SOUL.

The diversities of opinion upon this subject, may be reduced to four general views, of which one only can be true. These are briefly, as follows:

(1.) The view that *the soul is a material substance*, which like the body perishes at death. Some physiologists hold that what we call mental states are merely conditions or processes of the brain; that sensibility is "the special property of nervous tissue," and that "there is no necessity for supposing the existence of an immaterial substance, under the name of intellect or soul." Some mental philosophers, like David Hume, without asserting that the soul is material, come to the same conclusion with the materialists, that whatever may be its substance or modes of action, so far as a distinct *consciousness of ex-*

istence is concerned, the soul like the body, is dissolved by death.

(2.) The second theory of the soul is quite the reverse of this; viz., that *immortality is an inherent property or attribute of the soul,* and that the soul exists under a law of progressive development, which will lead it onward and upward from stage to stage and sphere to sphere of an unending existence. This view denies that the present is a state of probation to be followed by a state of retribution, and that the soul needs a moral renovation by supernatural power to fit it for heaven. This idea of immortality is that " the essential element of man, the principle of individuality, never dies;" his personal identity never ceases; but he grows in knowledge, in virtue, and in happiness, by a law of nature pertaining to the soul itself. Of this view the late Theodore Parker was a prominent representative.

(3.) A third view of the soul is that at his creation *man was endowed with immortality conditionally;* " created not absolutely immortal, but in a certain sense *for* immortality; i. e., immortality was his natural and proper destination,"* but that he has forfeited the boon by sin, and can regain it only through Christ. This is the view of those who believe that the souls of the wicked will be annihilated after death. They hold that Christ " not only reveals, but *bestows* immortality," and therefore, that all who do not embrace Christ will die, in the literal sense of a destruction of their individual being.

(4.) A fourth theory is that the soul of man *is endowed by the Creator with the property of immortality;* that therefore it will never cease to exist—each individual soul retaining its personal identity and its consciousness forever;—that evidence of this is given in the light of nature with sufficient clearness to have gained the assent of thoughtful minds in all ages; that the Jews derived this belief from their Scriptures, and were sustained in it by Christ; and that Christianity reassures

---

* See Dobney, Whately, and Hudson.

men in this natural and ancient belief by bringing the fact of the immortality of the soul, and the characteristics of the future state, out of the region of speculative inquiry and prophetic intimation, into the broad clear light of revealed knowledge.

If we can establish this last view as correct, the preceding theories must fall to the ground without further argument. A question so momentous to Job in the early meditative age of the race and in the quiet of Arabian deserts, and no less momentous to Paul in the height of Roman civilization and amid the pomp and stir of the world's capital, a question that engaged the profoundest thought of Plato and had a most emphatic prominence in the teachings of Christ—is alike momentous to every one of us, who now tread the shore of that great sea of existence upon which Job and Plato and Paul have launched, and where the Son of Man still walks in light.

> Here in a season of calm weather,
> Though inland far we be,

> Our souls have sight of that immortal sea,
> Can in a moment travel thither
> And see the [Blessed] sport upon the shore,
> And hear the mighty waters rolling evermore.*

Shall my soul live forever? Where? How? Am I immortal? And what shall be my immortality? He who thinks not of such questions, has the gift of reason in vain.

In discussing the question of the immortality of the soul, it is well to premise that such a fact does not admit of absolute demonstration. A mathematical demonstration—such as that the three angles of a triangle are together equal to two right angles—does not admit the possibility of a doubt. But moral and metaphysical subjects do not admit of measurement by lines and angles, or of calculation by numbers; and therefore, in the very nature of the case, it is impossible by moral reasoning to demonstrate a problem in morals in the same sense in which we demonstrate a problem in mathematics. Yet we can rest upon a conclusion of moral reasoning

---

* Wordsworth altered.

with no less confidence than we rest in a mathematical demonstration. I am just as sure that George Washington was the first President of the United States, and that Warren fell at the battle of Bunker Hill, as I am that two and two are four; yet the process by which I reach the conclusion is very different in the two cases. The greater part of our beliefs and actions are based upon moral reasoning, and not upon mathematical demonstration, or absolute knowledge.

(1.) With respect then to the soul, its existence and its properties, I remark that *Consciousness gives us the fact of an existence distinct and different from material objects, and having qualities, states, and modes of action of which matter is incapable.*

There is in every person the fact or phenomenon of consciousness. This consciousness is to each person a revelation of his self-hood and its properties. We *know;* we *feel;* we *think;* we *remember;* we *choose;* and we are *conscious* that we do know, think, feel, remember, choose. But all these facts, phenomena, processes, which we recognize through consciousness, must belong to some *substance;* there must be a something that thinks, knows, feels, remembers, wills. This is evident from the continuous repetition of these phenomena, as manifested through one and the same consciousness. This something we call mind, soul, spirit,* and we attribute to it qualities, properties and acts which are impossible to matter. Matter has extension, weight, solidity; but we do not measure mind by the inch or the square yard, we do not weigh it by the ounce, we do not conceive of it as spread over a given surface. On the other hand matter does not reason, or soar upon flights of imagination, or exhibit moral sentiments and affections. These phenomena which consciousness reveals we attribute to a substance distinct from matter, which we call mind, or the soul. We cannot go behind these facts of consciousness. We make this

---

* I use these terms as popular synonyms, without noting the distinctions which philosophy has made between them.

distinction in all our conceptions, in our laws, and our modes of speech.

I see a Japanese upon the street; my eye takes in his form, and I get an impression of his individuality, though I do not exchange with him a single thought. But at the same instant my thought flies thousands of miles to his home in Japan. I picture to myself millions of Japanese, their country, their manners, their institutions; and the mind contemplates the empire of Japan, which the eye has never seen. Nothing of that material organism which pertains to me goes to Japan, nor could go there under ninety days. Matter does not think nor imagine; and thus through consciousness we arrive at the existence of a *self* which is not material.

Again, this thought of mine in its swift flight to Japan and back, suffers no collision with air, earth, or sea; encounters no obstruction; has no sensation such as the material body would have by contact with another. The mind experiences no physical sensation in forming an idea or receiving an impression of an object, however large or distant. Mind and thought are immaterial; the soul-substance is a something distinct and different from matter.

Human language proves this to be the belief of mankind. You cannot translate the words Soul, Spirit, Mind, into terms denoting material objects, without making nonsense of human speech. Take two or three expressions of the Bible, simply as language. "Then shall the dust return to the earth as it was, and the spirit return to God who gave it." How would it read to say, "and the *brain* shall return to God who gave it"? Stephen cried, "Lord Jesus, receive my spirit!" How would it sound to translate this into the language of materialism, and make the dying martyr pray, "Receive my *brain!*" If we believe in God at all, we believe in him as a Spirit. Now "the Spirit of God beareth witness with our spirit, that we are the children of God." How would it sound to say, "The Spirit beareth witness with our *nervous tissue*, or our *sensorium*, that we are the children of

God"? I do not speak of the shock that such a substitution of terms would give to the sentiment of reverence, but of the nonsense it would make of human language. And the fact that the terms of materialism cannot be applied to the soul without absurdity, proves that human language herein represents the consciousness of man that the soul is not a material organ, but a distinct spiritual substance.

This argument from language is finely presented by Auguste Nicolas, in his *Etudes Philosophiques sur le Christianisme.** After describing the identity of the natural phenomenon of dissolution as it appears to the senses, in man, in the beast, and in the plant, he asks, "How comes it then, that in the heart of that universal destruction amid which we live, in that sepulchre of our mortal life wherein we are immured, the idea of our own immortality has penetrated—rather has germinated and flourished? Why is it that no one thinks of attaching this idea to the or-

---

* Fourteenth edition, Paris. Vol I., pp. 127, 132.

ganic or vital principle of a plant or a beast, and that every one, almost without hesitation, attaches it to the vital principle of that other *mortal*, which we call man?

"And then, how is it that to himself alone man applies the adjective *mortal?* This seems in the highest degree to contradict the idea of his immortality. In a world where all is *mortal*, he reserves for himself alone this qualification, as if all were *immortal* except himself. It is because the reverse of this is true, and therefore he alone needs to remind himself that in one sense—namely, as to his body—he is *mortal*. . . . . We have no consciousness of our existence except through the immediate perception of a subject in which it is essentially summed up, and which we call ME. This Me we can conceive of only as a *simple* being, whence we conclude that it is *immaterial*. It is the highest expression of indivisibility and unity." Such is the first fact of consciousness, with its necessary deductions.

All criminal law is based upon the same

distinction. The nerves and muscles that communicate from the brain to the arm the motion that strikes a man dead, are precisely the same whether that blow is struck by an insane person or by a wilful assassin. But if one kills another by the act of a diseased brain, we do not count him a criminal, but send him to an asylum. Yet the same physical action directed by an intelligent will is murder. We attach moral action and responsibility only to the soul as a conscious personality. If sin is disease, there is no such thing as guilt.

(2.) *This conscious substance which we call the soul, in distinction from the body, has a continuous personal identity.*

It is always the same soul, day after day, year after year. In each case it is the *one* being who has been the subject of the various thoughts, emotions, experiences of a life-time. Each person has a past, which belongs to himself. It is not merely that such and such thoughts and feelings have run through his brain as through the hopper of a mill; but these thoughts and feelings belong to him as part of his personal history. The acts of former years he remembers as his acts ; the sins of former years he remembers as his sins, and with a present sense of guilt, if they have not been repented of and forsaken. The suspension of consciousness, as in sleep, does not destroy this personal identity, no more than stopping the pendulum of a clock destroys the substantial reality of the clock and its machinery. The man who has been unconscious in sleep for eight hours, or through the days of a fever, wakes up the same man, conscious of his personal identity. "Destroy identity, and you destroy the individual."*

> This frame, compacted with transcendent skill,
> Of moving joints, obedient to my will ;
> Nursed from the fruitful globe, like yonder tree,
> Waxes and wastes—I call it *mine*, not ME.
> New matter still the mould'ring mass sustains,
> The mansion changed, the tenant still remains.†

The proof then that the soul exists as a spiritual substance distinct from matter, is

---

* *Les Horizons Célestes*, p. 152.   † Brown.

drawn from the testimony of Consciousness to acts, states, and properties which do not pertain to matter; the universality of this consciousness as shown in the terms of language for such a thinking, feeling substance; in the distinctions of criminal law; and in the consciousness of personal identity, which does not rest upon the form and particles of the body but in the acts and memories of the mind. What spirit is we cannot define. What the substance of the soul is, and how separate from the body, it is impossible to say. We fall back upon the testimony of consciousness—and our highest philosophy of the soul is expressed in that short catechism which an English wit invented to satirize our ignorance. "What is mind? No matter. What is matter? Never mind. What is the soul? It is immaterial."* Still man is conscious of his preëminence over the animal creation; and this not merely as a higher kind of animal, a more perfect organization of phosphate of lime, iron, and albumen,—

* Punch.

but as another sort of being, having a resemblance to the animal only in the frame-work which the spirit inhabits. In many ways mankind assert their belief in the existence of the soul as the ground of superiority in man over the animal creation.

(3.) *This belief in the existence of the soul as a distinct substance having personal identity, is shown in the special attention given to the education of the mind.*

The domestic animals are trained with care for certain offices. But this training lies wholly within the limited range of certain well-ascertained instincts. When it goes beyond this, when the imitative faculty in certain animals is exercised upon functions more properly human, this is regarded merely as a matter of curiosity, and not at all as a sign of intelligence and progress. No one thinks of opening a school for animals because here and there one is trained to pick out the letters of the alphabet; or of communicating knowledge to them through the medium of language. Instinct and imitation do not rise to the level of reason, or furnish a basis for mental development. The animal does not appear to originate ideas, or to form plans by the process of deduction and analysis, but only to follow the routine of instinct from one generation to another. The horse, the mule, the ant, the bee, the lion, the coney, have made no change in the habits of life, and no progress as tribes or orders of the animal creation, since the days of Solomon and of Job. The natural history of these animals is the same to-day that it was thousands of years ago.

But man is a subject of education, and of that progress which education stimulates; and by the general consent of mankind, education is made a duty of the family and of society. Now why is this preëminence assigned to man? Is it merely because he is superior as an animal that man must be educated? But many animals have individual members or points of organization in which they are superior to man. Some are superior in strength, others in agility, others in swiftness, or power of locomotion; though none possess the combination of powers possessed by man. There is some higher difference between men and beasts than in their physical organization. It is not merely the different way in which bone and muscle are put together, or the relative proportions of earthy and fleshy matter, that make man worthy of an education that beasts cannot receive. True, education increases the value of man as a working animal. Knowledge increases the average of human skill; but it were not worth the pains and cost of educating men, if they were mere animated machines.

In education we look for the development of mind as the grand result. The pains taken in the instruction of the deaf and dumb and the blind, is warranted by the belief that within the imperfect bodily organization there resides a soul-substance capable of development and enjoyment, though hindered from the highest spiritual manifestations through material forms. The wonderful achievement of patience and skill in the edu cation of Laura Bridgman, who is deaf, dumb, and blind, not only excites admiration as a curiosity of science—it touches and thrills the heart with sympathy, because within that defective and unsightly physical organization is found a soul capable of the thoughts, desires, affections, hopes of a spiritual being. A consciousness, a personal identity, a moral sense were brought to light within those dark and silent chambers. Her teacher thus describes the effect when after protracted efforts with raised labels and single letters, which could be distinguished only by the sense of touch, some glimmering of conscious thought appeared within a mind that had never known the joy of sight, nor the melody of sound or speech.

"Up to this point the process had been merely mechanical, not materially differing from that under which a knowing dog may be taught a variety of tricks. The poor child sat in mute amazement, and patiently imitated everything her teacher did. But now the truth began to flash upon her; her intellect began to work; she perceived that there was a way in which she *could herself make up a sign of anything that was in her own mind;* it was no longer a dog or a parrot; it was an immortal spirit, eagerly seizing upon a new link of union with other spirits." Who will not acknowledge that here were evidences of a soul-substance, having consciousness and identity? Who can believe that this is of the earth, earthy? The whole system of education, intellectual and moral, belies such a belief.

One may be trained, as an animal, to skill in a particular department, without being educated in general knowledge. Why then is man so educated, and why is his education felt to be of so great importance? Why must we have schools, colleges, books, journals, apparatus, and all the appliances of mental improvement? Is it merely that the material resources of the earth may be developed, and the comforts and luxuries of life increased? Is it that man may rate higher in political economy as a producer, or as a labor-saving machine? Nay, nay; all this stir for education as a matter of duty and of right for the masses of men, is the voice of man's spiritual nature, proclaiming his superiority as a being to the beasts that perish. It is the moral and the spiritual in man asserting its superiority over the physical and the economical; it is the protest of humanity against the skepticism that denies its relations to God and to the spiritual world, and degrades it to the fellowship of beasts.

(4.) *The same assertion of the self-hood of the soul as a substance having personal identity is seen in the existence of those laws and moral restraints that recognize man as a responsible being.* Men do not frame laws for brutes. Laws are made for the owners of beasts, regulating their management with reference to the interests of human society; but for brutes themselves men make no ordinances. But from the cradle to the grave man is the subject of law—in the family and in the state, and of the unwritten law of society. In the framing of laws, in the punishment of crime, men recognize in human nature a principle of intelligence and responsibility not imputed to brutes. The whole system of laws, political and social, gives the lie to that philosophy which allows to man no pre-eminence in kind over the beast. We do not charge brutes with crime. They may be unmanageable, refractory, revengeful, dangerous; they may require restraint and punishment; sometimes the public safety demands that an unruly animal be put to death. But we never charge dumb beasts with criminality, even in the destruction of human life. But when men do mischief to their fellows we charge them with crime, and hold them amenable to law. If an ox gore a man to death we call it an accident, a calamity; it may be expedient to kill the ox, but we do not try, condemn, and execute it, as a criminal. But if a man wilfully take the life of his neighbor he is a criminal, and must be dealt with as such. Now, why is this difference? Criminality requires intelligence—the reasoning faculty and a moral sense—the capacity to distinguish right from wrong. And herein mankind universally concede to each other this bad pre-eminence over the brute—that human nature can do a moral wrong, which brute nature cannot. If then it be denied that man has a personal soul, with moral qualities and affections, a subject of moral government, I affirm that the whole framework of human society, the whole system of laws and punishments, is built upon just the opposite idea. "Without personal identity I comprehend neither heaven nor earth—every relation disappears."*

Men treat one another as moral and responsible beings; as having something more than the instinct of brutes;—a higher nature knowing good and evil, for whose acts they are accountable to law. The difference thus recognized between man and the brute is not a mere difference of material organization; it is an essential difference;—the difference between a rational soul and animal instinct. Who can believe that a being for whom is

* *Horizons Celestes*, p. 151.

arranged the stupendous framework of law and its sanctions—after a short career of mere animal sensations passes into nonentity like the beasts that perish? Has man no pre-eminence above the beast? Is all vanity?

(5.) *There is no evidence of the cessation at death of that conscious existence of the soul whose identity is unbroken through life.*

The suspension of consciousness in sleep does not interrupt the identity of being in the sleeper. Dreams and the illimitable flights of imagination of which we are conscious in whole or in part during sleep, prove that the mind is not bound by the chains that hold the bodily senses in suspense, nor paralyzed by the inaction of the will. In death the body sinks into a rigid repose, in which motion and sensation and every sign of vitality and of consciousness disappear. After death the bodily organism is dissolved and its elements pass into other forms, but there is no evidence that one particle of matter is annihilated. We do not see the spirit die, nor any indication of decay and dissolution in the mind, while the body is dying. Every fatal disease or accident produces in the body one uniform result—the cessation of animal existence. Whatever the manner of dying or its proximate cause, the event is marked by the same phenomena; the blood ceases to circulate, the lungs cease to heave, the muscles cease to move. But there is no such uniformity in the manifestations of the spirit upon its approach to death. Sometimes mental manifestations are obscured or impeded by the condition of bodily organs in disease. But often when the body is wasted to the very verge of dissolution, the mind exhibits its highest vigor, in the extacy of love, hope, and joy, or the energy of fear and despair. Often the soul watching the sure approach of death in the body, asserts the consciousness of its own existence unimpaired. "I still live," said Webster as he watched the tide of physical life ebbing out from his stalwart frame. The *I*—the personality of the man—asserts its consciousness amid the dissolution of nature. As the shipwrecked traveler sees all his treasures go down into the deep, and stripped even of his apparel, breasts the breakers, and comes shouting to the shore, so the soul naked as it came from God, leaves the wreck of the body, and strikes out for the shore beyond, exulting that it lives ;—or perchance is cast upon that shore lamenting that it could not die.

There is not a single fact connected with the dissolution of the body that proves that the soul is disorganized by death. A *post-mortem* dissection can trace every organ and tissue and fibre of the body, but it finds no remains of the spirit, and no trace of its entrance or exit. No microscopic physiology has been able to detect the source of life, or the seat of the soul. If the telescope of the astronomer should fall and break to pieces, we would not infer that his eye had lost the power of seeing because a mechanical help to sight was gone. If the strings of a musical instrument should break, we would not infer that the musician had lost his faculty of combining sounds or his skill to play. But what is the eye to the soul but a telescope, a mechanical contrivance for conveying impressions to the inner sense? And what is the voice to the soul but a musical instrument by which it utters its own thoughts and emotions? The soul will get impressions though the eye is blind; the mind will express thought though the tongue is dumb. When the eye sleeps in death, does the soul die? When the lips are sealed, has the spirit ceased to be?

But here it is alleged by way of objection, "that the faculties of the mind are often impaired by disease, intemperance, old-age, and that all evidence of the existence of such faculties terminates at death."

With reference to the first class of facts the *want of uniformity* detracts very much from their weight in the argument. Though it is true that some diseases seemingly impair the faculties of the mind as well as the powers of the body, this is not true of *all* diseases; it is not true of many diseases that prove to be mortal; it is not always true, of the same dis ease. In certain diseases the reflective powers remain in full vigor till the very moment of death. Perception, reason, imagination, memory, are all in active and perfect exercise: the mind exhibits the utmost power of analysis, and the most distinct and accurate apprehension of whatever is brought before it; the current of the affections is full and strong; and the highest mental enjoyments and sufferings are experienced even till the latest breath. Sometimes even all former mental experiences are surpassed in vigor and vivacity at this critical moment. Is it credible then, that when through the whole progress of a disease for weeks or months the faculties of the mind have not been in the least impaired by it, the final termination of that disease should suddenly destroy those powers, and annihilate the mind which at the very instant of death possessed the full vigor of life? Do not facts of this description teach us that " the mind is not *so* dependent upon the body as necessarily to decay, languish, and die under the causes that destroy the body."

Disease often impairs and deranges the action of the mental faculties. But is there any proof that it *destroys* the mind? When the cause of the derangement is removed is not the mind restored to its wonted activity? What is there in such phenomena to warrant the belief that the mind may be destroyed by any of the causes that temporarily affect the body? The want of uniformity in the effects of disease upon mental manifestations, takes away entirely the force of the objection.

The same may be said of the effect of old age and its attendant infirmities upon the mental faculties. This is by no means uniform. The action of the mind is not *necessarily* dependent upon the vigor of the body. Often in fact the mental powers will seem to be more lively and energetic by contrast with the weakness of the body; like a steam-engine in a frame-work too feeble to support it, which sways and rocks with every motion of the piston. In fact there are instances in which the body seems to be a mere *incumbrance* of the mind, so that the mind becomes more etherial in its manifestations, more like pure spirit, as the crevices of its crumbling case reveal more distinctly its essential force.

The loss even of very important organs of the body does not in the least impair the vigor of the mind. As Bishop Butler so ably remarks;—" With regard to our power of moving or directing motion by will and choice; upon the destruction of a limb, this active power remains, as it evidently seems, unlessened; so that the living being, who has suffered this loss, would be capable of moving as before, if he had another limb to move with It can walk by the help of an artificial leg, just as it can make use of a pole or a lever, to reach towards itself and to move things beyond the length and the power of its natural arm; and this last it does in the same manner as it reaches and moves, with its natural arm, things nearer and of less weight. Nor is there so much as any appearance of our limbs being endued with a power of moving or directing themselves; though they be adapted like the several parts of a machine, to be the instruments of motion to each other; and some parts of the same limb, to be instruments of motion to the other parts of it.

"Thus a man determines that he will look at such an object through a microscope; or being lame, that he will walk to such a place with a staff a week hence. His eye and his feet no more determine in these cases than the microscope and staff. Nor is there any ground to think they any more put the determination into practice, or that his eyes are the seers and his feet the movers, in any other sense than as the microscope and the staff are. Upon the whole, then, our organs of sense and our limbs are certainly *instruments*, which the living persons, ourselves, make use of to perceive and move with. There is not any probability that they are more; nor, consequently, that we have any other kind of relation to them, than what we may have to any other foreign matter formed into instruments of perception and motion, suppose into a microscope or a staff (I say any other *kind* of relation, for I am not speaking of the degree of it,) nor consequently is there any probability, that the alienation or dissolution of the instruments is the destruction of the perceiving and moving agent."

The fact that the action of the mind is sometimes impaired by bodily disease cannot be urged with reason against the existence of the soul after death, since this is not the uniform effect of disease, and very great changes in the physical system often produce no visible effect whatever upon the mind.

The obscuration of the mental powers is not their extinction. There are cases of recovery to the full vigor of mental action from a state of insanity prolonged through many years. There have been cases also of the restoration of consciousness after a long suspension of it in consequence of a blow upon the skull or a disease of the brain. Eclipse is not annihilation.

But it is urged that in death we lose all evidence of the soul's existence. True. But the want of evidence of its existence is not to be taken as proof of its non-existence. The utmost that can be affirmed from this phenomenon is that we no longer *know* that the soul exists; we surely do not know that it does *not* exist. There are parallel phenomena which shed light upon this point. Suppose we had never seen or known *sleep;* and now for the first time drowsiness steals over the frame, one by one the living powers lose their activity, till the whole man sinks into unconsciousness. The eyes are closed, the ears are heavy, the lips are silent, the limbs are motionless, and nothing but the gentle heaving of the breast and the scarce perceptible motion of the breath indicate the presence of life. We gaze with wonder at the mysterious change. We call to the sleeper, we move him, we try in every way to rouse him, but in vain. We watch with painful solicitude for some new development. At length sleep relaxes its hold; the spell is broken; the stupor passes off; the man awakes to consciousness, with freshness and vigor. Sleep being our habit we do not regard it as mysterious; yet is it not, as an ancient called it "The image of death?" In sleep not only is the active exercise of our powers suspended, but all capacity of exercising them for the time being is suspended also; "and yet the powers themselves remain undestroyed;" so that we are not re-created every morning, but are the same beings when we wake—with the same consciousness, the same personal identity as when we went to sleep.

The same thing occurs in swoons, when for a considerable period all evidence of the soul's existence is withdrawn, but nevertheless the soul continues to exist and manifests its wonted activity as soon as the physical obstruction is removed. Drowned persons also have been resuscitated and restored to consciousness after all evidence of the existence of the soul had ceased.

Death destroys the organs of sensation and all the functions of animal life. But the continued existence of the mind does not depend on these. In a certain sense we may be said to exist even now in two distinct states—a state of sensation, when we receive pleasure or are in any manner affected through the senses; and a state of reflection, when independently of the senses, we reason, remember, and experience either mental pleasure or pain.

In dreams the mind is often able to recall ideas of objects, persons and scenes, to reason, plan, decide, without the use of the senses. Indeed, the mind seems at times to leave the body and to revel in distant spheres. What evidence then is there that death destroys the soul? There is not even a presumption against the continued existence of the soul in any of the phenomena connected with death.

Nicolas argues that "suicide itself, that fearful abuse of the dominion of the soul over the body, is a strong proof of the distinction in their destinies. Can the power that kills be the same that is killed? Must it not necessarily be something superior and surviving? The act of the soul which in that fatal instant, is in one sense so great an act of power, can it at the same time be the act of its own annihilation? The will kills the body; but who kills the will?"*

(6.) The argument is strengthened by the fact that *man has the capacity of believing himself immortal; has a native expectation and desire of immortality, and shrinks from it only because of sin.* Even the most barbarous tribes worship the spirits of their ancestors and believe in some form of existence after death. The Egyptians preserved the body from decay, believing that in the remote future the soul would return to its forsaken tenement. With the Greeks and Romans the souls of heroes were canonized as having entered the abode of the gods, and the Manes, the spirits of the dead, were had in reverence. The higher minds in Greek and Roman philosophy—Socrates, Plato, Cicero, and others, distinctly argued the immortality of the soul. And though their reasoning may be unsatisfactory to us, yet as Jeremy Taylor

* Etudes, Vol. I., p. 134.

says, "they cast out every line, and turned every stone, and tried every argument; and sometimes proved it well, and when they did not, yet they believed it strongly; and they were sure of the thing, even when they were not sure of the argument." The state of the argument of ancient philosophy for the immortality of the soul is well put by Addison in his familiar soliloquy—

> "It must be so—Plato, thou reason'st well!
> Else whence this pleasing hope, this fond desire,
> This longing after immortality?
> Or whence this secret dread, and inward horror,
> Of falling into nought? why shrinks the soul
> Back on herself, and startles at destruction?
> 'Tis the divinity that stirs within us;
> 'Tis heaven itself, that points out an hereafter
> And intimates eternity to man."

The citations from the Greek and Roman classics given in the first lecture, proving the belief of the ancients in a future state of rewards and punishments, of course exhibit their belief in the immortality of the soul as the conscious subject of those rewards or punishments. The argument of Socrates as preserved both by Plato and by Xenophon in various detached conversations, may be concisely stated to the following purport—

The soul has a capacity and a desire for knowledge beyond what it can attain in this present life. Here we know nothing of *things*, but only their phenomena, their motions, their changes, and the like. But the human mind is not satisfied with this merely relative and finite knowledge. It seeks for something higher and nobler. It aspires to grasp the absolute and the infinite, to comprehend things in their essence as well as their attributes, to know events in their causes as well as in their connections and their order; in a word, to penetrate into the depths of being, and there, beneath the ever-varying appearances, to recognize and apprehend the unchanging realities upon which these depend. This, however, it can never do, so long as it remains shut in on all sides by the body, with no other inlets to knowledge than consciousness and the five senses. Moreover, our progress in knowledge is continually hindered by the body, by its diseases and infirmities, its passions and lusts. How then shall the end for which the soul was made be accomplished, if its existence ceases with death? From all this Socrates inferred that good men would continue to exist after death, would pass into a higher state of being, and would become perfect in wisdom and in happiness.

Plato himself uttered similar sentiments, of which perhaps the most remarkable is this, in the Phædo: "If death were to be the dissolution of the whole, it would be good news to bad men when they die, to have an end put to this body and to their depravity, and also to their souls; but since the soul appears to be immortal, there is no other way of escaping evil, no other safety, but to become as good and as wise as they can."* It is not claimed that these pagan philosophers held such views with entire consistency, or advocated them with the weightiest arguments. Sometimes doubts and fears outweighed argument and hope; sometimes notions of preexistence or of transmigration marred the

* Phædo, 130.

simplicity and force of the plea for the immortality of the soul. But still we trace in the ancient philosophy that undying instinct and reasoning which is the soul's mute prophecy of an Hereafter.

At a later era, Plutarch seems to assume the immortality of the soul as an accepted fact. "Since the soul exists after death, it is probable that it partakes both of rewards and punishments; for in this life the soul is in a state of conflict, like a wrestler, but when it has finished its conflict, it receives suitable retributions."*

Herodotus was of opinion that the doctrine of immortality originated with the Egyptians.† But traces of this belief are to be found in the literature of almost every nation of antiquity. Even Bolingbroke concedes that " the doctrine of rewards and punishments in a future state, began to be taught long before we have any light into antiquity; and where we begin to have any, we find it

* De Sera Numinis. † B. xi. c. 122.

established;" that this doctrine was "strongly inculcated from times immemorial;" and there are traces of it as far back as the most ancient and learned nations are known to us.*

The yearnings of affection toward the dead, the belief that they still live, the universal shrinking of the mind from the thought of their annihilation, are intimations of the soul's affinity with a world exterior to this in which the body lives and dies. There are insects whose antennæ are so delicate that the eye can hardly detect them; yet these articulated feelers are intensely sensitive. Sometimes the ear of the insect is at the base of such a feeler, and thus the slightest vibration of sound is instantly conveyed to the creature as a warning of danger or a suggestion to guide its movements. So the soul sends out its spiritual affections into the great unknown, and listens for some breeze or voice that shall convey to it an intimation of the immortal life. Love and Hope in the soul of man gravitate toward immortality.

* Fragment XXIX. Works, Vol. VIII. p. 60. See also Essay XLVI.

In view of the death of men and of beasts respectively, mankind instinctively pronounce a difference between man and the beast in nature and in destiny. And this universal sentiment, acting itself out in the event of death, is worth more than volumes of philosophy to teach what men really believe upon this subject. As I sat by the window of a country house overlooking a rail-road, the train came rushing by and horribly mangled a cow upon the track. For a long time the wounded beast lay there neglected, moaning in her pain. By and by, when neither her owner nor the workmen of the road appeared, a neighbor, moved with pity, put an end to her sufferings with the blow of an axe. Suppose that a man had been thus wounded, instead of a beast. Would he have been suffered to lie there for hours without sympathy or relief, because it was no one's business to care for him? How soon would intelligence of the accident have spread from house to house. Here you would see men running from their labor in the fields to make a litter to convey the sufferer to the nearest dwelling. There a farmer would get up his horse to go in quest of the village doctor. All would be sympathy and attention. But why all this stir over a wounded man, if man has no preeminence over the beast at death—if both sink into annihilation? If both are alike in their future, why make so great a difference in feeling and in conduct toward them in the same circumstances? No litter was brought for the cow; no barn or hospital was opened for her cure; no surgeon was called to inspect her wounds and try his skill in restoring her. Why this difference? Would it be because the man's life might be saved, and to prolong his life even as a cripple would be an act of humanity? But the same thing would be done if it were known that he must die. And suppose that the surgeon on examination of his wounds should declare that he must die in an hour. Would any one suggest that it would be an act of kindness to terminate his sufferings by a blow? But why not? To dispatch the beast with an axe was an act of pity;—but to strike the dying man with an axe, though it were certain that he would die within an hour, would be a crime. Now why is this, if man has no pre-eminence above the beast, and we do not know at death whether his soul goes upward or downward? Why this ado about a man more than about a beast, if both are alike of the dust, and return to the dust to live no more? Is it because man walks erect, and the beast upon all fours? Is it because man has a more finished structure, and a more polished skin? Is it because the lime, and the iron, and the silex, and the albumen, and other elements that enter into the structure of both, are differently graduated or compounded? Is it because the one is a common earthen vessel and the other a porcelain vase, that we feel so much the more for one than for the other when both lie hopelessly in pieces? No, no! It is because of the difference in the contents of those vessels—the one all of the earth, earthy; the other a spirit sprung from God himself. Let the man thus mangled and dying be the most wretched and worthless of his species; not worth keeping alive for any good he is to society; still we cannot look upon his death as we look upon the death of a beast. We do homage to the soul of a man. The soul is so great that it ennobles whatever pertains to it; and therefore we may not dishonor or defile the body, because of the soul—which, even in death, asserts its pre-eminence. The feeling here described is but another protest of humanity against that skepticism which in death would degrade it to the fellowship of beasts. We honor man above the beast in death, because we know that while the dust returns to earth, " the spirit returns to God who gave it."

(7.) *The faculty of conscience in the human soul argues its immortality.*

Man is rational and mortal. He acts freely; and his actions are good or bad according to a moral law. Conscience sits in judgment upon his actions, and gives him pleasure or pain in the review. But conscience is prophetic as well as retrospective. Conscience refers the soul to a standard and an authority above itself. Conscience suggests and foreshadows a retribution for wrong. Conscience points to the eternal justice, and often compels the soul to disgorge its secret crimes when death draws nigh, that it may prepare to meet God in the judgment. "Now this original justice, seated in the soul, the type and sanction of all the justice upon earth, itself has need of sanction, without which it could not have the existence which it communicates to other forms of justice. The idea of justice and of law can be conceived only through the idea of *commandment* and of *vindication*, and the idea of commandment and of vindication can be conceived only through that of *force* and *sanction*. A justice that one can violate indefinitely has no existence, it is a chimera. . . . . He who will not admit the immortality of the soul is forced to deny justice, morality, duty, conscience, God ; and by that denial, to sap the foundation of all society; for conscience and human justice have their value and position only through the conviction of a Justice infallible and supreme, of which these are the type; this Justice itself cannot be conceived of without the certainty of a full satisfaction; and it is demonstrated that this satisfaction does not here exist.

"Open now the gates of another life, and that sovereign Justice immediately appears, awaiting the just and the unjust, to render to each according to his works; justifying the patience of its delays by the inevitable power of its decisions, the moral disorder here by the necessary and praiseworthy play of our freedom, and establishing by its certainty the order of the world disturbed by its oblivion."* Would the soul be created with such a faculty as conscience, if it were to perish with the body?

(8.) *There are evidences of a moral government over the world, whose final results are not reached in the present life.* For what end is the discipline of the mind; its capacity for knowledge, its growth in knowledge, its un-

* Nicolas Etudes, pp. 151—3

ceasing thirst after knowledge, if man is like the beasts that perish? What mattered it that Newton's pet dog, playing in his study, spoiled the laborious calculations of the philosopher, if Newton was to die like Carlo, and to pass into nonentity? To what intent is the discipline of the soul under moral law, if virtue and vice shall rot together in the grave? Why should Paul press upward toward seraphic hights of excellence, if he and Paine must sink together into annihilation? Why have a moral government; a law of right; a conscience; a sense of justice and of sin—if the most unequal distribution of good and evil in this life winds up the scene forever? Why build so grand a theatre of moral action, and bring Virtue, and Hope, and Law, and Religion upon the stage, if the curtain is to fall and the lights be put out, when the Devil is the hero of the play?

Look at a mind like that of Chalmers, or of John Foster, maintaining its own discipline with unabated force, putting forth its energies upon the highest themes of humanity without one symptom of flagging or decline, kindling and swaying other minds with its own fresh and vigorous creations;—doing this up to the moment of retiring at night, and in the night alone and silently passing into the sleep of death;—can any man believe that this mind then ceased to be, merely because it ceased to *act* through the wonted machinery of the body? When John Quincy Adams, who had never betrayed the least failure of his comprehensive and versatile intellect, halted amid the very scenes of his life-long labors and triumphs, and lay down to die, was there not an assertion and vindication of the soul's undying nature, in that quiet but sublime contrast of the perishable body with the imperishable essence of the man? "This is the last of *earth*—I am content." Not the last of *me;* the *I*, the conscious personality, surveys "the last of earth," and is content. *Sic itur ad astra.*

Yet how many plans of wisdom and philanthropy are unfinished when a great and good man dies. How much of what he himself was capable is left unattained. Mere animals, so far as we can see, attain the full end of their existence and the full measure of their powers and capacities in this life. But who will affirm this of man as an intellectual being? Look at his progress in the conquest of nature—his ever-multiplying inventions, researches and discoveries, all leading to his own higher development. Look at the mariner's compass, the printing-press, the steam-engine, the telescope, the magnetic telegraph, the manifold products of human skill in seizing and applying the hidden principles and forces of nature, and tell me whether he who achieves such triumphs over matter, is himself only a material organism, made to eat and drink and die, and be no more! Ponder the reasonings of the human mind in philosophy and morals, its searchings after truth, its reachings forth into the infinite, its soarings as upon angels' wings into the very depths of heaven, and tell me, is the dissolution of this body the end of existence to that mind?

Our very birth is a type of the second higher birth, which we call death. Before entering upon this stage of life, the unborn infant had faculties and organs given it in anticipation of the condition in which it should be placed; organs of sight, hearing, speech, of respiration, digestion, locomotion, which, all useless and unsatisfied, yet were not superfluous; but were a mute prophecy of a higher life to come, and a preparation for a state of being as distinct as the butterfly upon the wing from the crysalis in the cocoon. And so the instincts and yearnings of the soul for some higher life, that "second sight" by which it seems even now to discern that which is invisible—those aspirations which nothing earthly can satisfy, a will and affections that tire not when the body sleeps, hopes full of immortality—are not these a prophecy of a higher stage of existence yet to come, and an adaptation to that existence, for which *sin* may indeed disqualify, but which *death* cannot destroy?

When thought has traversed all measurable

space, and the powers of instruments and mathematics are exhausted; when imagination, flying upon the wings of the morning, alights upon the utmost verge of the material creation:

> Then still the *heart* a far-off glory sees,
>   Strange music hears;
> A something not of earth still haunts the breeze,
>   The sun and spheres.
>
> All things that be, all love, all thought, all joy,
>   Sky, cloud and star,
> Spell-bind the man, as once the growing boy,
>   And point *afar*—
>
> Point to some world of endless, endless truth,
>   Of life and light,
> Where souls renewed in an immortal youth
>   Shall know the Infinite.

If there be not an existence for the soul after death, what a blank, a mystery, a mockery is man! And what a blank, a mystery, a mockery is that whole moral system—a system of truth, of law, of motives and principles grand and enduring as eternity—with which man is so evidently and indissolubly connected! Should that system, with results so unfinished, with issues so unsatisfac tory, wind up forever when death shall have depopulated this globe, could God remain an object of reverence and love to the holy angels?

(9.) *These arguments for the soul's immortality from the light of nature, are illumined and fortified by the teachings of Scripture.*

I know it is alleged that the Old Testament does not teach this doctrine. It does more; it assumes it, and illustrates it as a truth too deeply imbedded in the soul to call for argument. The book of Job is not all dark; the book of Ecclesiastes is not all dark; both give the freest scope to the speculations and fears of men concerning death and the grave, yet both lift the curtain and let in glimpses of the light beyond. Vainly does skepticism cull from these its proof-texts against the doctrine of immortality; such books are not to be judged by isolated texts, but as a continuous argument; and each, taken as a whole, is the answer of faith to skepticism.

Enoch walking with God and suddenly translated, Elijah going up to heaven in the chariot of fire—is there no life and immortality here? Does the New Testament make us any more sure of the existence of these worthies when it refers to them as living in another state, than the Old Testament left us, in describing the manner of their exit from the world? In the Old Testament, the spirit of man is contrasted with his physical organization, as being capable of intercourse with God, and subject to reward and punishment for moral action. Contrasts of character are drawn as affecting destiny. "The wicked is driven away in his wickedness, but the righteous hath hope in his death."* David contrasts the temporal prosperity of the wicked with his own hope of awaking in the likeness of God, to behold his face in fulness of joy. The attempt of rationalistic critics to limit this sublime hope to some change of outward condition, is extremely puerile. The Christian's hope, "full of immortality," can find no higher expression than this lofty faith of David. When the Scotch martyr, Alexander

---

* Prov. xiv : 32.

Hume, stood upon the scaffold, he said, "Farewell all earthly enjoyments; farewell my dear wife and children—dear indeed unto me, though not so dear as Christ, for whom I now suffer the loss of all things. And now, O Father, into thy hand I commend my spirit. Lord Jesus, receive my soul." Here was the specific faith of the Christian, clearly and satisfactorily expressed. But the martyr had yet more to say. When the fatal cord was adjusted to his neck, he sang in a clear, full voice, from the good old Scotch version:

> But as for me, I thine own face
> In righteousness will see;
> And with thy likeness, when I wake,
> I satisfied shall be.

The words of David the singer of Israel gave to this Christian martyr his song of victory over death. Had David no faith in immortality? Do words which rung as a heavenly chime from the scaffold of a Christian martyr, and are felt to be the highest possible expression of Christian faith and desire, become dumb and meaningless—or which is far worse, earthly and carnal, when sung by the lips of their author? Not the most attenuated subtleties of logic and exegesis in the school of Rationalism, can rob these immortal words of their immortal life.

Both Isaiah and Daniel speak of the revivifying of the *body*, as well as the future consciousness of the spirit. "Many of them that sleep in the dust of the earth shall awake, some to everlasting life, and some to shame and everlasting contempt."* "Thy dead men shall live; together with my dead body shall they arise...... He will swallow up death in victory."† The force of these passages cannot be evaded by regarding them as figurative expressions, applied to the resuscitation of the Jewish nation. Every figure has a basis of fact, and what is that basis here, but the sublime fact of the resurrection of the dead, foretokened to the prophets of the old dispensation? And so of that heroic faith of Job, whether we interpret it of a literal resurrection of the body,

---

* Daniel xii. 2.   † Isaiah xxvi: 19.   xxv. 8.

or a spiritual resuscitation in the joyous recognition of God, yet the theme itself thrills the soul as a prophecy of immortality; and Handel could find no loftier expression of the full triumph of the believer over death, than these exulting words of the patriarch: " I know that my Redeemer liveth—and though this body be destroyed, yet *after* [or out of] my flesh shall I see God."*

The belief in a future state of rewards and punishments was almost universal among the Jews in the time of Christ. No surprise was expressed by them at his teachings upon that subject. Christ never argued the immortality of the soul; nor did he propound it as a new and strange doctrine; nor is there any evidence that it was so received. Assuming it as a familiar truth, he set it in a clearer light from his own knowledge. It was already an article of orthodox faith among the Jews, rejected only by the skeptical sect of the Sadducees. Paul took advantage of this circumstance in his defense at Jerusalem. When

* Job xix : 25.

he perceived that one part of the council were Sadducees and the other Pharisees, he cried out, "Men and brethren, I am a Pharisee, the son of a Pharisee; *of the hope and resurrection of the dead* I am called in question. And when he had so said, there arose a discussion between the Pharisees and the Sadducees; and the multitude was divided. For the Sadducees say that there is no resurrection, neither angel nor spirit; but the Pharisees *confess both*."* At this appeal, the Pharisees at once declared for Paul. Again, before Felix, Paul claimed that the doctrine of the resurrection, instead of being a heresy of Christians, was a part of the orthodox faith of the Jewish nation, derived from their law and prophets; " believing all things which are written in the law and in the prophets; and have hope toward God, *which they themselves* [his accusers] *also allow*, that there shall be a resurrection of the dead, *both of the just and unjust*."† Likewise before Agrippa, Paul asserted the doctrine of the resurrection

---

* Acts xxiii : 6—9. † Acts xxiv : 14, 15.

as embraced in " the promise made of God to the fathers."* It was not as a new tenet broached by Christ, that Paul preached the resurrection; but he argued the credibility of the resurrection of Christ, from the fact that the doctrine of the resurrection of the dead was taught in the Sacred Scriptures of the Jewish nation. This Paul affirmed before the Sanhedrim and in hearing of multitudes of the Jewish people; and only the sect of the Sadducees, the rationalists of that time, would deny his statement. How common among the Jews was the belief in a future existence and in the resurrection of the dead, is evident from the reply of Martha to Jesus when he said to her, "Thy brother shall rise again." So far from expressing surprise, as if this were a novel and incredible suggestion, she calmly answered, " I *know* that he shall rise again *in the resurrection at the last day.*" It is impossible to account for this wide-spread belief among the Jews, unless we apply to such passages as have been cited

* Acts xxvi : 8.

above from the Old Testament Scriptures, the spiritual interpretation of Paul, which finds "in the law and the prophets," and in the promise given to the fathers, the high and blessed doctrines of the resurrection of the dead and the life everlasting.

But it remained for the Gospel to clothe the realities of the future with the certainty and precision of outline that *light* imparts. Christ " abolished death." Surely he did not abolish the fact of death as a physical event; but for all believers in his grace he abolished its penal effect and its accompanying gloom and terror. He " brought life and immortality to light." He did not for the first time reveal a future existence; but with the certainty of knowledge, he so discoursed of the condition of the soul after death as to make that condition as clear as day. This is the strict interpretation of the participle in the text— φωτίσαντος, *illuminating*, making clear or light. The phrase " life and immortality " is strictly " life and incorruptness," which is equivalent to an imperishable life. Paul exhorts Timothy not to shrink from the afflictions which the service of Christ would bring upon him; not to be ashamed of the testimony of the Lord, or afraid to avow himself the friend of the imprisoned apostle; but to look beyond bonds and afflictions, and death itself, to the salvation which God having given us in his own purpose "before the world began," has now "*made manifest* by the appearing of our Saviour Jesus Christ." And Christ by his teaching and by his own death and resurrection, has rendered death powerless or null as against believers, for whom he has illuminated the future with the promise of everlasting felicity in his kingdom.

Christ himself recognized the future existence of the soul as a doctrine of the Old Testament. When the Sadducees questioned Jesus as to the resurrection he replied, "Ye do err, not knowing the *Scriptures.*"* 'Your own Scriptures should have taught you the spirituality of the future life.' What Christ revealed was "not *that* there is a life to come

* Mat. xxii : 29.

and a future state, but what each individual soul may hope for itself therein, and on what grounds." He made manifest through his redemption a life of incorruptible and eternal blessedness, as a subject of promise, an object of faith and hope. *This* life he gives to believers. But Christ never represents mere existence after death as his boon. He describes the wicked as existing after death, Dives as well as Lazarus—the hypocrites as well as the righteous appearing in the judgment. And for these is reserved not annihilation but punishment; not progressive restoration but eternal retribution.*

Away then with the gross notions of the materialist; the dreamy speculations of the rationalist; the gloomy retreat of the annihilationist. MAN IS IMMORTAL. The fact of his immortality is unalterable. But the tenor of that immortality will be such as himself shall here decide. Stupendous thought! Upon your will as the point of a needle, vibrates an eternal state, and two worlds

* Mat. xxv : 31–46. See Lecture VIII.

tremble in the balance;—a card, a dice, a gilded toy, may turn the scale downward to hell;—a prayer of penitence, a cry of faith and love, may draw down heaven and make it yours. You *are* immortal; your soul will live forever and ever. But how and where? You know that without holiness it cannot see the Lord. Christ offers to redeem and save you—and death impends—and THE FOREVER comes!

Does death seem dark? Sin makes it dark. Has the future terror? Sin makes you afraid. Look to Jesus, and all is light. Commit your soul in faith to him, and you will be able to say with Paul, "I know whom I have believed." Your life of faith and holy love being "hid with Christ in God;—when Christ, who is our life, shall appear, then shall ye also appear with him in glory."

LECTURE VII.

ETERNAL PUNISHMENT A DOCTRINE OF THE BIBLE.

2 Thessalonians i: 7–11. *When the Lord Jesus shall be revealed from heaven with his mighty angels, in flaming fire taking vengeance on them that know not God, and that obey not the Gospel of our Lord Jesus Christ; who shall be punished with everlasting destruction from the presence of the Lord, and from the glory of his power; when he shall come to be glorified in his saints, and to be admired in all them that believe.*

This passage, upon the face of it, teaches these things:—That the Lord Jesus who here suffered and died for the salvation of men, shall one day appear from heaven in visible power and glory;—that at that appearing he will publicly and in the most impressive way, discriminate as a judge between those who by faith in himself have led holy lives, and those who have rejected the knowledge of God, and have not obeyed the Gospel of Christ; that in that day, believers or saints shall share in the glory of their Lord; but the ungodly or unbelieving shall be visited with judicial retribution and everlasting destruction, proceeding from Christ himself.

This revelation or manifestation of Christ from heaven will be a distinct and notable event. It is spoken of in the New Testament as "the day of the Lord,"* "the day of God,"† "the day of the Lord Jesus Christ," "*that* day,"‡ his appearing; his coming. "Waiting for the coming of our Lord Jesus Christ, who shall confirm you unto the end, that ye may be blameless in the day of our Lord Jesus Christ."§ "The day of the Lord so cometh as a thief in the night."‖ "Look-

---

* 2 Peter iii : 10.   † 2 Peter iii : 12.   ‡ 2 Timothy iv : 8.
§ 1 Cor. i : 8.   ‖ 1 Thess. v : 2.

ing for the glorious appearing of the great God and our Saviour Jesus Christ."*

This is an event;—not a succession of manifestations, as when Christ summons individual believers into his presence at death, and thus in a sense manifests Himself to them; but one signal event, *an appearing of Christ*, marked by such signs in heaven and earth as have never before been witnessed. "The day of the Lord will come as a thief in the night; in the which the heavens shall pass away with a great noise, and the elements shall melt with fervent heat; the earth also and the works that are therein shall be burnt up."† "The Lord Jesus shall be revealed from heaven, with his mighty angels."‡ Christ will then appear as sovereign and judge; clothed with the authority of the Father, attended by the angels of his power, "he shall judge the quick and the dead at his appearing and his kingdom."§

In that day, at that coming, the Lord Jesus

* Titus ii : 13.   † 2 Peter iii : 10.   ‡ 2 Thess. i : 7.
* 2 Tim. iv : 1.

will discriminate between two classes of men, according to his Gospel. His saints, those who have believed upon his name, and by faith in Him have separated and sanctified themselves from the world, shall then enter into their final rest and glory. In this all who accept the Scriptures as authority are agreed. But on the other hand, he will execute judicial wrath upon those who have rejected God and the Gospel of his Son. Upon this point the language of the text is as explicit as it is terrible. The objects of the Saviour's righteous indignation are distinctly specified. Those "who know not God"*—a phrase descriptive of moral condition; a wilful ignorance, a blindness through sin; a disregarding God as He is manifested in his works and his word; and "who obey not the Gospel of our Lord Jesus Christ"†—who disregard the provision of grace and salvation through Him;—these are they in *character*, who shall receive retribution.

This retribution will be inflicted in the

---

* 2 Thess. i : 8.   † 2 Thess. i : 8.

form of judicial punishment from Christ himself; and it will be everlasting in its duration. These two points command our special and earnest thought.

I. *The penalty that shall be visited upon the ungodly and unbelieving in the day of the Lord Jesus, will not be the mere penalty of natural law, but a judicial punishment, inflicted by Christ himself in his capacity of Sovereign and Judge.*

This feature of penalty distinguishes a moral government from a mere natural system of development. Natural laws have their penalties. It is the nature of fire to burn, and the nature of flesh to feel pain when burnt with fire. When therefore a man puts his hand into the fire and suffers pain, this is according to the laws of nature; it is not a judicial infliction of punishment for his rashness—the pain follows as a matter of course. When a man commits a crime against his fellow,—steals his property or takes his life, it is natural that he should feel the inward smarting of remorse. In proportion to the healthy and normal action of conscience will be the strength and pungency of these self-upbraidings for crime. This is the law of his nature. He may partially arrest or evade its action— for conscience makes itself felt only through consciousness; it acts from within, through reflection and the sensibilities of the soul; and one may partially drive off reflection by business, by society, by travel, by sensual pleasures, or may stupefy consciousness for a while by drinks or drugs. But neither trade nor talk, neither the dance, nor gin, nor opium can reverse the law of nature so that the consciousness of a crime distinctly contemplated as crime shall give pleasure in that act; nor can any of these outward devices and appliances so break the law of nature that when left to itself again conscience will not give pain for crime. But this is the law of nature, and unless interrupted it takes effect as a matter of course, without any interposition from the author of nature. But when the murderer is arrested for his crime, tried and sentenced to be hung, he suffers the judicial penalty of that law of the community which he has violated; and this is not the mere natural sequence of wrong-doing, but an authoritative testimony against wrong-doing, in the name of the law which is outside and above the criminal's own nature, but to which he is amenable as a member of society.

This obvious distinction between penalty as a natural sequence of violating law, and penalty as a positive infliction by judicial sentence, is of great importance in the question now before us. In both cases the pain is *penalty;* it comes through the violation of law. But in the one case the penalty merely brings out the relation of the offender to *a system of laws;* in the other the infliction of penalty brings into the foreground a *government* whose authority has been violated, and whose power is now put forth to vindicate that authority and to sustain its laws.

The murderer may suffer all the penalty of natural law and yet suffer no judicial penalty for his crime. He may elude the officers of justice, and yet feel such pangs of remorse that he cannot eat nor sleep. He may flee into the desert where no writ will ever pursue him, and yet be pursued forever by the phantom of his victim, so that all the sand of the desert shall be stained with the blood, and the drear silence of the desert be broken with the cries of that murdered man. All the horrors of remorse he daily endures as the penalty of his own outraged conscience. And yet justice is not satisfied, nor can be till the escaped murderer is brought under the condemnation of that law of society which he has broken. And to whatsoever island or rock or desert the murderer shall flee, there *this* penalty will overhang him still, waiting for his arrest and condemnation. The voice of universal justice finds utterance in that exclamation of the barbarians of Malta, when they saw the viper fasten itself upon the hands of Paul.—"No doubt this man is a murderer, whom, though he hath escaped the sea, yet vengeance"—that divine retributive justice which is above man and over man—"suffereth not to live."* The natural penalty in the inward gnawings of remorse does not meet the demands of justice for some public vindication of the violated law.

So on the other hand, the murderer having steeped his soul in crime, may steep his senses in liquor, and so stupefy conscience and allay its pangs, and thus escape awhile the natural penalty of his guilt. But the strong arm of the law may seize him, and he may be tried, convicted, and condemned to suffer the judicial penalty of death for his crime against life. Then the *law* is vindicated, even though to the last he hardens himself to his fate, and chokes down remorse by a profane and hideous mocking at death.

These two forms of penalty therefore—the *sequence* of natural law and the *positive infliction* of justice—are widely distinct. True, since God is the author of man's being and of those laws which encompass him as a nature, we may find even in the necessary penalty of natural law evidences of his moral indig-

* Acts xxviii: 4.

nation at sin. But penalty which comes as the mere sequence of natural law, without divine interposition, cannot fully meet the demands of God's moral law when violated by sin.

There are those who regard these natural sequences as the only penalty of sin; and who argue either that men will become inured to these pains, or that the penalty will work its own cure; and thus both the sin and the penalty become, in the ordinary development of law, a means of reformation. But we have seen that sin is the personal act of a free and therefore responsible agent, who is amenable not only to an inward law of his own nature, but to a law which is around him and above him, emanating directly from the throne of God. *That* law can be vindicated only by a judicial penalty, coming not in the way of mere natural sequence, as pain follows fire, but inflicted as a positive expression of the lawgiver's authority.

Society does not say of the murderer, 'Poor fellow, he has brought upon himself penalty enough in the torments of conscience; let him go where he will, he cannot be happy; we leave him to the working of natural law, till remorse shall issue in repentance.' No: society says, 'This crime against life must be punished by a penalty which shall fitly express the value of life, and shall guard its sanctity against passion and violence.' This penalty is not revenge; it is the necessary exponent of the law; and no matter what the murderer suffers in his own conscience, this *visible* infliction of penalty, by judicial sentence, by authority of the law, is due to every sacred interest of society and man.

And how shall God honor and uphold that moral law which is the life and order of the universe, except by some positive expression of his supreme approbation of obedience, and his supreme disapprobation of disobedience, in the form of rewards and punishments which can be *distinctly* traced to his authority as the giver of that law?

The punishment that shall be adequate to the expression of God's displeasure at sin, which shall demonstrate that God so loves the purity and happiness of his moral creation, that he will guard these against the possible triumph of evil, must be not some secret pain or fear in the bosom of the transgressor, nor some mechanical effect of law, nor some mere sequence in the order of nature, but a positive, visible, felt, recognized infliction of penalty from God as Sovereign and Judge. Precisely this is the form of penalty which the text declares—the visible infliction of retribution upon the ungodly, proceeding from the presence of the Lord, and from the glory of his power.

The vengeance threatened is not personal revenge, but judicial retribution. The word is to be taken in the old English sense of a just punishment for wrong doing, which is the exact idea of the Greek word $\delta\iota\kappa\eta$ in the text—JUDICIAL PUNISHMENT. God does not indulge toward the transgressor that feeling of malice and vindictiveness which we call revenge; but he *avenges* the evil done in his kingdom, by inflicting upon the transgressor the penalty of the law.

And as if on purpose to show that this penalty is not vindictive, nor out of harmony with love, but proceeds from benevolence itself, it will be pronounced by the Lord Jesus Christ in his own person as the final judge. The Saviour of men, he who died in human flesh that he might win men to the life of God, HE shall be revealed from heaven in flaming fire, executing judgment upon the unbelieving and the ungodly. This fact alone must suffice to cut off all hope from those that die in their sins. They will not only suffer the natural evil consequent upon transgression; they will not be merely dropped out of the fellowship of the good into some obscure and unknown fate; they will be publicly judged and publicly condemned; and this not by the mere natural operation of law, but by a direct and most conspicuous decision from heaven; and this too, will not be the arbitrary fiat of invisible power, but the official and pronounced judgment of Him who once appeared in the flesh to take away sin. The sentence of death will go forth from Him who appeared upon earth as the very embodiment of divine love and compassion; from Him who has done all that divine love could do to save the lost; it will go forth upon those who have refused the saving knowledge of God, and have disregarded the gospel of his grace; it will go forth after pardon has been offered and refused; after Christ has been preached and rejected; this sentence of eternal death will proceed from Him "who only hath immortality." The most poignant woe of that sentence will be that it expresses "the wrath of the Lamb." The utmost conception of a hopeless condemnation is given in that phrase. He who with the promptings of infinite love came forth from that throne in sight of all heaven, and became the Lamb of sacrifice, who from that throne has since dispensed his government of grace, will then commit himself before the universe to the punishment of those "who obey not his Gospel." The penalty of violated law and of rejected grace will be publicly pronounced by Christ himself. As the subjects of that penalty look forth upon the drear ocean of eternity,

> There is no ark of safety more,
> There is no distant sun-bright shore.

2. For the second great lesson of the text is that *the punishment which shall be decreed by Christ himself upon the ungodly will be eternal in its duration.*

After our thorough discussion of moral and legal principles bearing upon the whole subject of future retribution, the question of the duration of that punishment rests simply on the interpretation of Scripture. We have seen that there is no *à priori* argument against the doctrine of future punishment; that there is nothing in the character of God, in the principles of his government or the promises of grace, that render this doctrine incredible, or inherently improbable; but on the contrary, that the character of God and the principles of his moral government require that he should inflict the highest possible penalty for the transgression of his law. Let us sum up the several steps we have taken in this argument.

(1.) We have seen that the very nature of man, the constitution of the human mind, demands penal retribution for sin to satisfy its own sense of justice and of right. The laws, the religions, the literature of mankind unite their testimony to this principle of vindicatory justice, as deep and ineradicable in the bosom of the race. Conscience, I had almost said, is even more inexorable toward sin than God himself; for God out of the infinite fulness of his nature, has provided an atonement whereby He can pardon sin; but conscience can make no atonement, yet it demands that satisfaction shall be made for sin either through an accepted atonement or through penalty endured. When conscience is in its normal healthy state, it will suffer no peace in the mind till the wrong is made right, till justice is somehow satisfied, and right vindicated.*

---

* This line of argument is ably sustained by Prof. Shedd in his article on "The Atonement as a Satisfaction to Man's Ethical Nature." Bib. Soc. Nov. 1859.

And conscience certifies you that no moral obliquity with regard to sin, no plausible subterfuge for wrong will be allowed anywhere within its domain. In the darkest night when no human eye is upon you, when you can see nothing around you, conscience will bid you turn your eyes inward and backward, and she will light her candle and search every nook and corner of your soul for hidden sin, will brush away the cobwebs from your memory, and unlock your secret drawers, and touch every spring-door behind which evil has hidden, and will bring forth all your iniquity. Down in the bottom of your soul, under the accumulations of years, she will find some old dingy cast-away plate of memory, and she will hold it up and breathe upon it, and hold her light to it, and as the figures begin to stand out, will say to you—'*There* is your sin—*this* is what you did,'—and you will quake as did Job in his vision of the night.

Did you never do to another an injury for which death prevented reparation; and now when the memory of that act comes up after ten, twenty, thirty years, does it not shoot through you a pang as keen and unmitigated as when first you awoke to the consciousness of the wrong? For many years there was in the lunatic asylum at Philadelphia an intelligent and accomplished man, who, through his own untoward act, had made himself the victim of despair. He had killed his antagonist in a duel; but no sooner did he learn that his shot had taken fatal effect, than he abandoned himself to the horrors of remorse. Most pitiable it was to see him measure off the paces, stand and give the word Fire, then wring his hands and shriek, "He is dead! he is dead!" —then pace again, and fire, and renew his self-upbraiding. In that fatal moment when his victim fell, conscience took up her iron scepter, and smote down reason, and hope, and peace. So conscience "doth make cowards of us all."

And now as God is true, He who hath made you in his image, who has taught you by all these voices of your nature that sin ought to be punished, who has gathered up the verdict of the human race that sin must be punished, who has put you under the necessity of a satisfaction to justice for wrongdoing, if you would have peace in your own soul, this true and living God himself will punish sin and satisfy the requirements of divine justice and rectitude.

(2) We have seen also that the infliction of evil upon moral beings in this world, which is a universal fact of Providence, can be harmonized with the benevolence of God only by regarding this as a token and a warning of God's retributive justice for sin; so that the natural world is full of lessons of God's moral government by law and penalty.

(3.) We have seen also that the history of Israel proves that God, even though he is a Father, will fitly and fully punish sin.

(4.) We have further seen that Christ who has revealed God as a Father, teaches that he will punish the wicked forever.

(5.) We have seen, also, that God's special fatherhood over his believing people gives no warrant for the unbelieving to hope for protection and safety hereafter. The Scriptures teach that there will be a discrimination hereafter between the conditions of the righteous and the wicked, answering to the difference of their characters here. Common sense requires this. A preacher of Universalism was telling his little son the story of the children in the wood. The boy asked, 'What became of the poor little children?" "They went to heaven," replied the father. "And what became of the wicked old uncle?" "He went to heaven too." "Won't he kill them again, father?" asked the boy. The child's question opened to the father the absurdity of his doctrine of universal and indiscriminate salvation, and led him to renounce his belief in it.

(6.) We have seen, again, that the demerit of sin as against the law of love and the welfare of the universe, demands the highest displeasure of the God of purity and love. When that eccentric but honest man, John Randolph of Roanoke, lay on his death-bed, knowing that his end was nigh, he suddenly roused himself and shouted at the top of his voice, "Remorse! remorse!" He then insisted that the word should be written out distinctly, so that he could see it. Looking steadfastly upon the word, the dying man exclaimed, "Remorse! You have no idea what it is; you can form no idea of it whatever; it has contributed to bring me to my present situation; but I have looked to the Lord Jesus Christ, and hope I have obtained pardon." Here was a sense of the demerit of sin that made hell seem a necessity for all out of Christ.

Said a profligate young nobleman, whose last hours were witnessed by the poet Young, "My body is all weakness and pain; but my soul, as if strung up by torment to greater strength and spirit, is full powerful to reason, full mighty to suffer. Remorse for the past throws my thoughts on the future. Worse dread of the future strikes them back on the past. I turn and turn, and find no way." Ah! there is no way but by the cross of Christ, accepted here. For sin demands of

God the highest possible expression of his displeasure.

(7.) And we have further seen that if the grace of God in Jesus Christ is abused and rejected, there is no promise and no possibility of another probation or a final restoration of the condemned.

These principles settled, and the future punishment of the wicked proved, we are shut up to the simple declarations of the Bible touching the *duration* of that punishment. This forms the eighth and last proposition laid down as the basis of this discussion.

VIII. *The duration of the future punishment of the wicked cannot in anywise be limited by the mere fact of God's Fatherhood, as made known in Christ; but must be determined by the demerit of sin, of which God alone can judge, and ascertained by us from the declarations of the Scriptures, which reason can interpret.*

The demerit of sin, even as it appears to human reason when rightly exercised upon the law of love, is seen to demand the highest possible expression of God's displeasure. But the human mind cannot take in a full view of the enormity of sin. Only the eye of God can do this; and therefore, God alone can fitly measure and decree its punishment. That punishment he declares in his own word.

Now, with respect to these declarations, it is remarkable that upon the vast majority of readers they make the impression that the punishment of the wicked will be eternal. The immense majority of professed Christians agree in this view. The great majority of Biblical commentators and preachers hold the same view. And among readers of the Bible of all classes, by far the greater number get the same impression. This by no means proves the doctrine. I do not mention it for any such reason. But it is in evidence upon *this* point—the Bible *does make such an impression* on the human mind, and it is fitted to make it. This is apt to be the first impression of its language upon this subject, and the contrary belief is induced only by explaining away the first and obvious meaning of texts.

Why then does God use such language? We are told that it would be dishonorable to God's nature to inflict eternal punishment. Then the Bible dishonors God, for it does represent him as *intending* to punish the wicked eternally. Some tell us that all these representations of the Bible are the exaggerations of oriental imagery; and then proceed to pare them down and explain them away as meaning nothing. But is God given to *exaggeration* in his communications to his creatures? Could he not have told us plainly how much or how little he will punish the wicked? If he does not mean to punish men forever, why use a style of language which makes upon the common sense of the race the almost uniform impression that he will punish the wicked eternally?

Figures of speech do not always go beyond the reality they are designed to express. They often fall below it, and are multiplied because no simple form of speech can state the reality in all its strength. This is true of much of the imagery of the Bible with reference to the future state of the righteous; why is it not equally true of its imagery touching the future state of the wicked? Mr. Theodore Parker frankly admits that the Bible does teach the eternal punishment of the wicked, and assigns this as one reason for not receiving the Bible as a revelation from God!

Take the particular text before us: "Who shall be punished with everlasting destruction." A question is here raised by those who believe in the annihilation of the wicked. That question I shall discuss at length in the next lecture; but I may briefly anticipate the argument so far as to apply it to this particular word.

(1.) The idea of annihilation is inconsistent with many passages which represent the wicked after death as in a state of conscious suffering. The parable of Dives is here in point. We must take the *general consent* of Scripture upon the whole subject of future punishment, as a guide to the meaning of the word destruction.

(2.) If annihilation were here intended, what need would there be of the qualifying term? The *annihilation* of a being would of course be final and everlasting. If the destruction in its very nature reaches to the essence of the being, it is the merest tautology to speak of this as everlasting. The term destruction denotes a state of ruin, but does not of itself determine the form of that ruin. The destruction of one's character or hope is a different thing in form from the destruction of his property.

(3.) The word destruction, and every other term describing the future state of the wicked, harmonizes with the generic idea of misery; but other declarations concerning the future condition of the ungodly cannot be made to harmonize with the idea of annihilation;— therefore *misery*, not annihilation is the central and controlling thought in all these declaration.

(4.) *Un*figurative and *un*ambigious terms

in the Bible teach the eternity of future punishment. Not all the language of the New Testament on this subject is figurative. And where there are many figurative expressions touching a given event, and there are also literal declarations upon the same event, the *literal*, non-figurative passages determine the meaning of the figurative. This is the only sound principle of interpretation. I shall expand and apply it in the next lecture with reference to that determinative passage in Matt. xxv: 41—46. Leaving then, the annihilationists for the present, I would apply the argument from the text to another class of objectors.

Annihilation is not universal salvation;— the destruction of conscious being because of sin, is quite remote from the salvation of all men from sin. I am now reasoning mainly with those who believe in the continued existence of the soul after death; and the question relates to the *duration* of that punishment which the Bible declares shall come upon the wicked after the Judgment. This question hinges upon the word "*everlasting.*"

It is objected that this word is used in a limited sense. But its primary signification is that of unlimited duration, and where is the warrant in the subject or the context for limiting it here? We cannot limit words arbitrarily, to suit a philosophical theory.

The word (*aionion*) *does* express the idea of eternity as clearly and fully as does any word in any language. It is fitted to express this idea, and is often used in the most absolute sense as to duration. This is its natural meaning. It is *the* word of all in the Greek language which best expresses the idea of unending duration, and this is its first and radical meaning. Why is such a word used at all, if the design is to threaten only a limited punishment? An *indeterminate* duration is the starting point in the meaning of *aionion*, and it is used in the text without a semblance of reservation or limitation from any cause.

The word *aionion* represents the duration

of the life of believers. The decision which our Lord himself says that he will pronounce upon the ungodly, must be taken as determinative upon this whole subject:—"These shall go away into everlasting punishment, but the righteous into life eternal." The same *aionion* measures the duration of both states. Why then limit it in one clause and not in the other? Why did Jesus select this one particular word—the strongest term for eternity in the Greek tongue—if he did not intend to say that the punishment of the wicked will be as lasting as the blessedness of the righteous? The same parrallel is conveyed in the following words: "The Father loveth the Son and hath given all things into his hand. He that believeth on the Son hath *everlasting* life; and he that believeth not the Son *shall not see life;* but the wrath of God *abideth* on him.* The unbeliever shall never know the blessedness of the believer; but the punitive displeasure of God shall abide upon him. He upon whom the penal judgment of

---

* John iii : 35, 36.

God shall " abide," he of whom it is declared that " he shall not see life"—and this in contrast with that "*everlasting* life" which is promised to believers—shall surely suffer an unending, unmitigated penalty for his transgressions. In that day of glory and of power when He who was despised and rejected of men " shall come to be glorified in his saints, and to be admired in all them that believe," then they who have refused to acknowledge God and to obey the Gospel of Christ, shall be visited with that penalty of the law of love, which by the destruction of all hope and happiness, shall bring upon its subject a ruin without remedy and without end.

LECTURE VIII.

Punishment, not Annihilation, the Future Portion of the Ungodly.

Matthew xxv: 41 and 46. *Then shall he say also to them on the left hand, Depart from me ye cursed, into everlasting fire, prepared for the devil and his angels. . . . . And these shall go away into everlasting punishment.*

These words declare the most awful fact connected with the future state. No man who considers by whom they were spoken can be indifferent to their meaning. If the language is that of oriental hyperbole it is well to know that, and to strip it of imaginary terrors. If the language is accommodated to Jewish prejudices and notions, it is well to know that. If it is the language of simple sober truth, it is well that we should ponder its meaning; nay, it were madness to disregard it. Dare we then look, *can* we look over the dread abyss of eternity, and dropping our plummet many thousand fathoms deep, judge whether it strikes soundings at last amid the wrecks of annihilated being, or sinks forever in a sea without bottom and without shore? Dare we ask, can we know whether the guilty spirit without hope in Christ, driven from the bar of judgment, shall thenceforth cease to be, or shall suffer forever under the indignation of a holy God? No idle curiosity tempts us to that awful verge. No speculative spirit moves to such inquiries. The instinct of self-preservation; the natural desire of happiness; the natural fear of evil; the yearning of the soul for immortality; the voice of conscience, and the warning voice of Scripture—these all bid us look into that future and be admonished to escape in time *whatever* of evil may await those who die in their sins. Concerning that evil, its nature and its duration, we can know nothing but what God has chosen to reveal. What he has made known to us in his word we have already in part considered. But there remains a specific question to which recent discussions have given unusual prominence.

Does the Bible teach that the future punishment of the wicked will consist in the *annihilation* of their being or in a state of *conscious suffering?*

In pursuing this inquiry, it is important to settle at the outset the principles of interpretation by which we must be governed in an examination of the various texts that bear upon it. It is agreed upon all sides that many texts of Scripture referring to the future state of the wicked, are highly figurative. It cannot at the same time be literally true that they shall be consigned to a place of *fire,* to a place of *darkness,* and to a second *death.* Where we find such contrariety of terms used to describe one and the same event or condition, we perceive at once that each of these is used in a figurative meaning, to express more strongly some common fact or truth underlying them all. How then shall we interpret such language? We cannot take one of these figurative expressions—whichever happens to strike our fancy or to suit our philosophy,—and say *this* must be taken literally and the others made to conform to it; we can neither take all literally, for that makes contradiction; nor can we take one literally and shape the rest by that, for this again would be arbitrary; but we must try to get at the idea which all these figures represent in common, and which each enforces by its own peculiar image. How then shall we get at this common idea? Either by means of some other declaration which is plainly literal, in relation to the same subject, or by comparing the figures side by side, that we may discover *what* meaning harmonizes them all.

For example; suppose a criminal had just been sentenced for a capital offense, and you knowing that I had come directly from the court-room should ask me what his sentence was; and I should answer, with apparent excitement at the result; "Well, it is all over with him; they have put him into the fire; they have stretched him on the rack; they have made an end of him; they have put out his light; they have buried him alive." But *what*, you ask, confused by this contrariety of images, what is the precise sentence pronounced upon him? To this I reply, he is condemned to solitary imprisonment for life. Now you understand me to speak literally. There is no appearance of a figure here, and this literal statement furnishes a key to the understanding of all my previous figures. You perceive at once that one imprisoned in solitude for life, is buried alive; is shut up from the light of day and the sweet light of home and of society; that although a sunbeam may sometimes struggle into his cell he is shut up to an unbroken night; that an end is made of him as far as human society is concerned, as completely as if he were annihilated; that he is stretched on the rack of his own conscience, and consigned to the fires of remorse. Now all the figures that I used at the first become intelligible; and while no one of them conveys a literal fact, each of them does convey a terrible reality, not one whit exaggerated, concerning this man's doom. And now comparing these figures with each other you perceive that they all do harmonize in this—*the severity and the hopelessness of the condemnation* which has fallen upon the criminal.

The rule of interpretation in such cases is clearly this:—The words of any writer or speaker are to be taken in their literal and obvious meaning, unless in the connection or in the nature of the subject, there is some good reason for understanding them figuratively, or in some secondary sense. Where there are several passages relating to the same subject, and some of these are literal and others figurative, **the** *literal* statements must give the key for the interpretation of the figurative. .... Where there are several statements on the same subject-matter, all which are obviously figurative, no one of these should be separated from the rest and treated as if it were literal, and thus made to govern the interpretation of other figures, but the several figurative expressions should be compared side by side with a view to ascertain a meaning common to them all. And still further, the literal meaning that underlies every figure of speech should not be overlooked or set aside with the idea that a figure is a *mere* figure of speech. In the hands of a serious writer—one who seeks to inculcate truth and not merely to play upon fancy—a figure is always the representative of some *fact;* and is designed to set forth that fact in vivid colors, so as to arrest attention and fix the essential truth.

If therefore the future punishment of the wicked were described *wholly* in figurative language, it would not follow that there is to be no such thing as future punishment; no more than it would follow that in the case supposed, the criminal had received no punishment, if I had only described that punishment under the various images of a fire, a rack, perpetual darkness, and a burying alive, without adding the literal statement that he was condemned to solitary confinement for life. So far from a figure having no corresponding reality, it often happens that a figure fails to express the whole reality ; that it is not in the power of language to convey the full meaning of the reality ; and therefore some single features are seized upon and thrown out in figures to make a partial impression where the whole is impossible.

Thus—to repeat an example given in the last lecture—we feel that this is true in a great measure of the imagery used in the Bible to describe the future blessedness of the righteous ; that it is not in the power of language to convey to us any adequate idea of the nature of the heavenly blessedness ; and therefore, that a few bold and striking figures are seized upon to represent particular features of that state. This also may be true of the figurative descriptions of the state of the wicked after death ; that they show the poverty of language, not its power.

But we are not left to the interpretation of figurative expressions to ascertain the future condition of the wicked. The language of the text is not figurative. It is a clear, calm, deliberate statement of what will be the future allotment of the righteous and the wicked respectively after death. It is a declaration from the lips of Christ himself, who will then be the Judge, and who will award to both the righteous and the wicked their final portion. This declaration, therefore, must be taken as fundamental to a correct understanding of the Scriptures on the whole subject. The figurative language of other passages must be interpreted by this exact and literal statement.

Our first and main inquiry therefore is, what is the meaning of these words of Christ? "These," *i. e.* the wicked, "shall go away into everlasting punishment?" The Greek word κόλασις (*kolasis*) here translated *punishment*, occurs but once elsewhere in the New Testament in its substantive form. We cannot therefore quote a wide range of New

Testament usage to assist us in fixing its meaning. There can be no doubt, however, as to its meaning in the other case. In I. John iv : 18, we read, " there is no fear in love ; but perfect love casteth out fear, because fear hath torment." The word *kolasis*, here rendered *torment*, is the same that in the text is translated punishment. It is not possible here to attach to the word the sense of annihilation. "Perfect love casteth out fear ; for fear hath *annihilation ;* he that feareth is not made perfect in love." If fear annihilates his being, of course he is not and never can be made perfect in love ; but what sense would there be in such a declaration ? The apostle is contrasting the effects of love and of fear upon the mind. Perfect love casts out fear; the love of God removes all apprehension, all disquietude from the mind ; for fear has torment, produces painful apprehensions concerning the future, and keeps the mind in a constant state of agitation. Paul speaks of those who through fear of death were all their life-time subject to bondage: Fear gives distress.

Plainly "torment" and not annihilation, conscious suffering and not a state of unconscious nothingness, is here the meaning of *kolasis*.

Again; although this word occurs but twice in the New Testament as a noun, the same root is found once as a verb, and once as a participle. In Acts iv : 21, we read of the Sanhedrim in their trial of Peter and John, "When they had further threatened them, they let them go, finding nothing how they might *punish** them, because of the people." The Sanhedrim had not the power of life and death; they could only chastise and imprison; therefore it would be absurd to say "finding nothing how they might *annihilate* them, they let them go." *Punish* is clearly the right translation of the word. Does it then mean anything else in the only remaining passage —II Pet. ii : 9. "He hath reserved the unjust to the day of judgment to be punished?" (*kolazomenous*.) Plato uses the same partici-

---

* *Kolazo* is the verb here used.

ple to describe one subjected to corrective punishment.*

These three are the only instances besides the text, in which the word *kolasis* in any form occurs in the New Testament; and it seems plain from these that it admits only of the idea of punishment, and does not once approach the idea of annihilation. The " torment," or painful disquietude that fear produces in the mind is not annihilation; fear is an intensely conscious, active, agitated state of mind; the " punishment" that the Sanhedrim sought some pretext to inflict upon Peter and John was not annihilation; the unjust are reserved for "punishment" until the day of judgment; why, then, should we not understand the same word in the text to mean *punishment*—something that a rational and conscious being will suffer?

If we turn from the New Testament to inquire the meaning of this word in common Greek usage, we shall be led to the same con-

* Gorgias 505 C.

clusion. We find the word in classic writers before the time of Christ, used to express the idea of *correcting, punishing*, but never that of destroying. Thus it is sometimes applied to a tree; where the meaning is not to cut down and destroy the tree, but to *prune* it, to curtail it by lopping off branches. The same meaning is transferred to the penalties of the civil law; and so the word signifies to correct, to chastise, to punish. Thus Plato says, "No one punishes the unjust because he has been unjust, but for the sake of the future, that he may not again do unjustly."* But how could one be reformed in the future, if he were annihilated? Plato uses the same word that Christ uses in the text; and he clearly means not annihilation but punishment.

The primary sense of *kolasis* is either "pruning" or "restraint"†—authorities being

* Protagoras 324 B.

† Prof. Tayler Lewis, to whom I am indebted for some valuable suggestions as to this word, regards this as the first sense of *kolasis*— 'restraint, holding, stricture." Hence the word is "utterly at war with the idea of annihilation," since restraint implies a subject

somewhat divided as to which phase of the idea that underlies both these words had precedence. Both are equally removed from the idea of annihilation; and both convey substantially the same meaning, since pruning is a checking or restraining of a wild irregular growth. It is easy to trace the metaphorical sense of punishing from the radical idea of pruning or of restraining. Hence *kolazo* is defined as to mutilate, maim, lop off or clip, as a tree, crop, curtail, coerce, chastise, rebuke with words or deeds. Thus Plato in his Gorgias, applies this word to restraints imposed upon the passions of the soul with a view to its correction.

Callicles having made the shameless avowal that to be happy a man should indulge his desires without restraint, Socrates compares

---

capable of action. An eternal *kolasis* will be the eternal binding of the sinning soul, as " in chains of darkness." The negative words *akolasia, akolastos,* &c., denote " freedom from all restraint." This seems to favor the view that " restraint" is the primary sense of *kolasis.* An eternal restraint imposed upon the soul by the power of its Creator, is incompatible with the idea of the destruction of conscious being.

the soul of a libertine to a diseased body which needs checks and restraints to restore it to health. He then asks, "Is not to restrain one from what he desires, to *punish* him?" (*kolazein*) and he adds that "to punish (*kolazesthai*) the soul is therefore better than unrestrained indulgence" (*akolasia*); i. e., to curb or prune the desires of the soul, to bring it under a corrective discipline, is far better than to leave it unrestrained. Socrates continues, "This man here can't bear to be benefitted, and to experience in himself that about which we are talking, viz., *kolazomenos* —to be chastised (or corrected)."* In this striking passage, the word in question is used for restraining and corrective discipline, and the idea of annihilation cannot possibly be extorted from it.

Some of the earlier classic writers made a distinction between *kolasis* and *timoria*, using the former to denote a punishment inflicted for the correction of the offender, and the latter for a penalty inflicted to

* Gorgias, 505 B. and C.

satisfy the magistrate or the law. Thus Aristotle says expressly that "*kolasis* is for the sake of him who receives it; but *timoria* for his sake who inflicts it, that he may be sated."* The same writer uses the term *kolasis* for the punishment of household servants. Nothing can be farther from the idea of annihilation than this of punishment administered for correction. This idea of *correction*, however, does not always attach to *kolasis* even in the earlier Greek, while in the later Greek it seems to have quite faded away, and *kolasis* came to be used synonymously with *timoria*. We even have the phrase (*kolazein thanato*) to punish by death, where of course the idea of correction by punishment is wholly lost. Ammonius† in his dictionary of Greek synonyms defines one of these words by the other,

---

* Aristotle, Rhetoric, B. I, Cap. x : § 17. In Bekker's edition the passage may be found on page 36, 33.

† Ammonius de differentia ad finium vocabulorum ; τιμωρεῖσ- θαι μὲν γάρ ἐστι το κολάζειν. I am indebted for this reference and for many valuable philological suggestions, to President Woolsey of Yale College.

thus showing that in later Greek, *kolasis* had quite lost its earlier corrective import, and had come to signify *punishment* without regard to motive. This helps us to understand the use of the word in the Septuagint. No instance has ever been adduced from classic writers in which this word means annihilation or anything approaching to that idea. While on the other hand, the addition of the term "everlasting," in the text, precludes the idea of corrective discipline or any other limitation of the punishment.

Plato appears to have had in view correction and example as the main design of punishment, and to make little of the judicial vindication of law. In his Protagoras he says, that "for the natural or accidental evils of others no one gets angry, or admonishes, or teaches, or punishes (*kolazei*) them, but men pity those having such evils." He gives as examples, ugliness, or small size, or infirmity of body. "But if any do not have those good things which are cultivated by painstaking, instruction and exercise, but have the contrary evils, for these things indignation and punishments (*kolaseis*) and admonitions are in place. For if O Socrates, you will but think what is the meaning of *punishing* (*to kolazein*) *the unjust,* this of itself will teach you that men think virtue to be acquirable; for no one punishes (*kolazei*) the unjust having his mind turned towards this and for the sake of this, viz., that a person did a wrong— that is no one does, who does not like a wild animal take revenge (*timoreitai*) without consideration—but he who tries to chastise (*kolazein*) with reason, does not punish for the sake of the past wrong deed,—for he cannot make that which has been done, become undone—but for the future, that neither he himself [the person corrected] may again do wrong, nor another who has seen him chastised."*

In this passage Plato keeps up the distinction between *kolasis* and *timoria*, using *kolasis* to denote punishment inflicted with a motive or for a reason, and especially for the

* Protagoras, 3235–3246.

discipline of the offender; and *timoria*, vengeance for a wrong committed. He seems to overlook the idea of a penal retribution for the sake of law, as belonging to *timoria*. But in many other passages Plato uses these words indiscriminately; and, as has already been remarked, the word *kolasis* lost all reference to the end of punishment, and was used to denote generically the infliction of punishment without respect to motive. Thus Xenophon uses *kolasis* and *timoria* as synonyms, with no difference of sense.† But *kolasis* never suggests annihilation.

The use of this word in the Septuagint confirms this view. A few examples will suffice. The Hebrew word in Ezekiel xiv: 3, 4, 7, which in the English version is rendered "stumbling-block," in the Septuagint is *kolasis*, that which makes liable to punishment. Again, in Ezekiel xviii: 30; "so iniquity shall not be your ruin, *kolasis*." The connection here refers to the threatened penalty of death.

† Cyrop, i: 2, 7.

The word occurs frequently in the Septuagint version of the Apocrypha. For example; in *Wisdom* xvi: 2, the writer speaking of some who were assailed by beasts says, "Therefore by the like were they punished worthily, and by the multitude of beasts tormented; instead of which punishment (*kolasis*) thou dealest graciously with thy people."

Wis. xix: 4, "Destiny made them [the Egyptians] forget the things that had already happened, that they might fulfil the *punishment* (*kolasis*) which was wanting to their torments."

The writer using the same word, speaks of some who though punished in the sight of men, had a hope full of immortality. Wis. iii: 4. In 2 Maccabees iv: 38, the slaying of a murderer is spoken of as a *kolasis*—the punishment that he deserved. But even capital punishment is not regarded by men as the annihilation of conscious being. Again in 2 Mac. vi: 14, we read, "Not as with other nations, whom the Lord patiently forbeareth to *punish*, till they be come to the fulness of their sins." Here the word *kolasis* is applied to such judgments as in the providence of God are sent upon nations. The same use of the word is found in Josephus. (Ant. xv : 22.)

In these cases it is evident that although *kolasis* has lost the distinctive idea of corrective discipline, it retains the idea of *punishment inflicted upon a conscious sufferer*, and does not once suggest the thought of annihilation.

Sophocles in his glossary of Later and Byzantine Greek, defines *kolasis* by "punishment, torment, damnation." He refers to the New Testament, the Apostolic Constitutions, Clement, Justin, Ireneus, and other fathers. He also gives as a secondary meaning ; *hell*, and quotes from the Apothegmata Patrum this remarkable passage from Isidorus, vi. : "If I be cast into hell (*kolasin*) I shall find you under me." Here are the two ideas of consciousness in a state of future punishment, and of gradations in that punishment. *Kolasis* is used for the place or state of punishment in the future. It is clear then, that the word *kolasis* originally implied correction, as the motive of the punishment; that it then came to be used without respect to motive or result, to denote simply the fact of punishment; and finally came to be an exact synonym of *timoria*, which originally implied *vindication*, and then came to denote *penalty* in the general sense. BUT IT NEVER MEANS ANNIHILATION.

We find therefore that this word is fairly translated in the text, by the word *punishment*, according to its use elsewhere in the New Testament, in classic Greek, in the Greek version of the Old Testament, by the Jewish historian Josephus, and by the Greek fathers. Now we must bear in mind that our Lord here uses no figure of speech, but gives a literal statement of the future condition of the ungodly. It will be a state of punishment; *that is the radical idea;* and all the figurative terms, fire, chains, darkness, death, destruction, and the like, come under this generic idea to give intensity to some peculiar phase of that *punishment* which underlies the whole.

Thus when we read that the wicked will, "be punished with everlasting destruction from the presence of the Lord," and at the same time read of "the smoke of their *torment* as going up for ever and ever," it is obvious that these representations are not to be taken *literally*, for then it would be impossible to reconcile them. One could not be annihilated as to his conscious being, and at the same time be in torment for ever. Both statements cannot be literally exact. Nor, since both representations are made by the same pen of inspiration, can we take one as literal and reject the other altogether. We must endeavor to harmonize them around some common idea. That idea is given by the Saviour in the text. He uses a phrase that cannot be taken figuratively; and which can surely mean nothing less than intense, unmitigated, and enduring *punishment*.

Take now that one idea, which is literally and explicitly conveyed by the words of

Christ, and examine in the light of it the figurative expressions of the New Testament touching the future state of the wicked; you will find that, as in the supposed case of the criminal imprisoned for life, every figurative representation of his doom is interpreted by the letter of his sentence. Are the finally impenitent said to be tormented in the flames, to be cast into a lake of fire and brimstone? This denotes not a literal burning with material fire, but a *punishment* so intense that it is like devouring flames. Are the wicked said to be chained in darkness for ever? This does not comport with living in the blaze of a fiery lake; but it does comport with the gloomy and hopeless nature of their *punishment*. Are the wicked said to be delivered over to destruction and to the second death? If this is taken to mean literal destruction of conscious being, then it does not comport with what is elsewhere said of their being in torment, their *dwelling* with everlasting burnings. But it does comport with the idea of a punishment that so completely deprives one of good, and shuts him up to his own wretchedness, that with respect to every blessing of existence he has ceased to be. And the Scriptures expressly define this, and not annihilation, to be the second death. " The fearful and unbelieving, and the abominable, and murderers, and whoremongers, and sorcerers, and idolaters and all liars, shall have their part in the lake which burneth with fire and brimstone; which *is the second death.*"*

To sum up all these in a few words; we find in the New Testament various representations of the future condition of the wicked which cannot be reconciled with each other if we take them *literally,* and which must therefore be understood in a figurative sense.

But a figure of speech has always underlying it some literal fact which it is designed to represent; and the idea common to all the terrible imagery of the New Testament concerning the future state of the wicked, is that of *complete and overwhelming evil ;* and this is declared by our Lord in explicit terms,

* Rev. xxi: 8.

when he says, "These shall go away into everlasting punishment." This is a literal statement; the word used means *punishment* and not annihilation; and there is nothing in any figure of speech, elsewhere used, to contradict this idea, but everything to enforce it.

If now we search the Scriptures with the eye upon the literal truth couched in figurative expressions, we shall find numerous passages describing the future condition of the wicked, that cannot possibly be harmonized with the notion of annihilation, but which all agree with the idea of *punishment,* in a state of conscious misery. These passages have been grouped together by Dr. Jonathan Edwards,[*] so as to form an argument of irresistible force.

"According to the Scriptures the wicked depart into everlasting fire. The smoke of their *torment* ascendeth up forever and ever. The shall *weep* and *wail* and *gnash their teeth.* They have no rest day nor night. The rich man in hell lifted up his eyes, *being in torments.* The wicked shall *dwell* with everlast-

[*] Works, Vol. I.

ing burnings. When the master of the house shall have risen up and shut the door, they shall stand without, crying Lord, Lord, open unto us; to whom the master shall say, I know you not, depart from me. After they themselves shall have been thrust out, they shall see Abraham and Isaac and Jacob, and all the prophets in the kingdom of God. The rich man in hell saw Abraham afar off and Lazarus in his bosom. The beast and false prophet shall be cast into a lake of *fire* and shall be tormented for ever and ever. The wicked shall be tormented with fire and brimstone *in the presence* of the angels, and *in the presence* of the Lamb.

"But how can those who are annihilated, be said to be cast into *fire*, into a lake of fire and brimstone and to be tormented there; to have no rest; to weep, and wail, and gnash their teeth; to dwell with everlasting burnings? As well might these things be said of them before they were created. How can they be said to *plead* for admission into heaven, and to *reason* on the subject with the master of the celestial mansions? How can they *see* Abraham, Isaac and Jacob in the kingdom of God? How can they, seeing Abraham and Lazarus in that state *enter into discourse* with the former? The smoke of their torments ascendeth up forever and ever, and they have no rest day nor night. But those who are annihilated, so far as they have anything, have continual rest day and night.

"The different degrees of the punishment of the wicked in hell prove that their punishment does not consist in annihilation. The punishment of the fallen angels does not consist in annihilation; and the damned suffer the same kind of punishment with them. In expectation of that full punishment to which they are liable they asked our Lord whether he were come to *torment* them before the time."

A living exegete of high authority, thus comments upon the use of figurative language touching the future state of the wicked.

"In the parable of the rich man and Lazarus, it may be conceded, that the fire in which this rich man is tormented, with the other drapery of the parable, is symbolical. Since he is a disembodied spirit, it would seem that it must so be understood. But the thing symbolized cannot be less terrible than the symbol itself. * * * * *

" In this parable *fire* is employed, in entire accordance with Jewish usage, as the symbol of *torment,* not of destruction : 'I am tormented in this flame.' No intimation is given that in this torment there is any approach towards annihilation. On the contrary his state of misery is represented as *fixed;* 'Between us and you there is a great gulf fixed ; so that they which would pass from hence to you, cannot; neither can they pass to us, that would come from thence,'— and there he is left." * * * *

" The final doom of the wicked is quite as often represented by the figures of *casting away,* as bad fish ; *casting out into the outer darkness ; shutting out of a feast ;* and with this very addition : 'there shall be weeping and wailing and gnashing of teeth ;' in all which passages the idea is manifestly *that of rejection and banishment from God's presence*, with the *misery* that accompanies such a condition, and this is *perdition* in the most awful sense of the word." *   *   *   *   *

"When our Saviour pronounces the sentence of the wicked ; 'Depart from me, ye cursed, into the everlasting fire which was prepared for the devil and his angels,' what could hearers understand, but that they should have their portion with the devil and his angels, and suffer the same punishment with them? If the punishment of the devil and his angels is, to be 'tormented day and night forever and ever,' what a strange and illogical conclusion to say that they who have their portion with them in the same lake, are to be, not tormented, but annihilated." *   *   *

"Eternal death, in the sense of banishment from God and all good with the misery naturally belonging to such a condition, is an intelligible idea, and that is also eternal punishment. Eternal death as the penalty of sin, in the sense of annihilation, is also an intelligible idea, but that would not be eternal punishment. The death itself (in the sense of non-existence) would be eternal, but the punishment would be its own limitation. It must cease when there was no longer a being to receive it. We can as well conceive of a man as punished a thousand years before he begins to be, as a thousand years after he has ceased to be."*

We have now fairly settled the meaning of one term in our Lord's final sentence of the wicked. He does declare that their portion after the judgment shall be one of *punishment*—of positive misery.

But another question is raised by some as to the *duration* of this sentence. It is claimed that the word translated "everlasting" does not always convey the idea of *endless* duration; but denotes an indefinite period. Now we readily grant that this word is sometimes used in a secondary and limited sense; to denote a period of the world, an age, or an indefinite time in the past or in the future;

* Prof. E. P. Barrows, in Bib. Sacra, July, 1858.

but wherever it is so used, there is something in the connection or in the subject to limit the term from its ordinary meaning. The question to be decided is, what is the common, natural meaning of this word *aionion*, and is there any reason to suppose that that meaning is departed from in the text?

1. What is the common, natural meaning of this word?

(*a.*) It is the only word in the Greek language that fully expresses the idea of perpetual duration. Plato and other classic authors use this word for endless duration or eternity as distinguished from the idea of time. It denotes the ceaseless course of things.

(*b.*) Jewish writers in the Greek tongue use this word for the idea of endless duration.

(*c.*) Out of a little more than seventy passages in the New Testament in which this word is used, in upwards of sixty it clearly expresses *eternal duration*. Many of these passages refer to the being of God; others to the happiness of the saints. This is the word and the only single word to express the eternity of God's existence, and the eternity of the blessedness of the righteous. This meaning of *eternity* is the common meaning of *aionion*, and is always its meaning in the New Testament unless there is something in the subject or the connection to limit it.

2. Is there any such limitation here?— There is nothing in the subject treated of that requires us to understand the word in a restricted sense. There is nothing in the nature of sin—for we have already seen that sin, being the rebellion of an intelligent being against the righteous government of God, and against the best interests of the universe, calls for the highest expression of God's displeasure—deserves his endless wrath.

There is nothing in the nature of God to limit this word; for we have seen that his benevolence requires that he should maintain the sanctity of his law, and inflict its utmost penalty for that end.

There is no promise, no, not so much as an intimation in the word of God, to limit the duration of future punishment. So far, therefore, as the subject itself is concerned, there is no reason for limiting in this place a word which in its common use is *un*limited.

Is there any such limit in the connection in which the phrase stands? On the contrary that connection settles the meaning beyond all question, as eternal. It is the same word precisely that is used in the same verse to denote the eternity of future blessedness:— " These shall go away into *aionion punishment;* but the righteous into life *aionion.*" The separate conditions of the righteous and the wicked will run on, and *on* and ON, in lines parallel but never approaching,

While life and thought and being last,
Or immortality endures.

If one shall cease the other will cease also. If the punishment of the wicked here described as everlasting is not to last forever, then the life and blessedness of the righteous, described by the same word as eternal, will not last forever. Awful as the conclusion is, we are shut up to the literal meaning of the Saviour's words, " These shall go away into *everlasting* punishment." Think what it must be to go *away* from Christ; to go away from his love, his glory, his blessed presence; to go away under his condemnation; and all the fearful imagery of chains and fire and darkness, of the undying worm and the tormenting flame, is verified by this one sentence of " everlasting punishment."

Of whom are these awful words pronounced? *Who* are they that, in the day of judgment, shall be sent away into everlasting punishment? They are those and *all* those who in this world have slighted Christ and his cause; all who in this world where good and evil, Christ and Satan are in conflict, have not enlisted fully, openly, heartily, on the side of the good—have not joined themselves to Christ in true discipleship. Christ is in the world as your Redeemer to claim your homage and your service. Christ is in the world in his cause, in his people, in his word, in the institutions that commemorate his death and his resurrection; in forms diverse and manifold Christ is appealing to you for love and for devotion. If you slight his call, if you withhold your heart, withhold your time, withhold your means, withhold yourself, squander your talent or bury it in a napkin, then he will say to you, "Inasmuch as ye did it *not*"—did nothing for me; did not accept my grace; did not enter my service; did not help my cause; but opposed me or stood aloof, therefore, "depart from me, ye cursed, into everlasting fire, prepared for the devil and his angels."*

Who says this? Who utters this awful condemnation? This is no raving of ignorance or fanaticism; no boast of vindictive cruelty; no figure of rhetorical fancy. All these words fell from the lips of Christ, the gentle, loving son of God, the friend of sinners. They fell from the lips of him who came into the world that, through faith in himself, men should not perish but have everlasting life. They mean all that the cross means; for it was because the Saviour knew

* Matthew 25 : 41.

the awful eternity that is before the wicked, that he died to redeem us from hell. Ah, these are Christ's own words, and therefore do they take away hope.

And *why* did he utter them? That you and I might fear; that you and I might flee! —might fear the just punishment of our sins; might flee from the wrath to come! That you and I might turn from sin; that you and I might come to him and through his cross gain everlasting life. Not to affright our souls with images of horror, not to distract our fancy with exaggerated terrors, not to excite our nerves at the expense of reason, not to put into the hands of priests and religious enthusiasts and demagogues an instrument of terror to govern the weak; no, no, not for any such reason as *they* allege, who deny future punishment, did the Son of God, the friend of sinners, the meek, the gentle, bleeding, dying Lamb of Calvary, give us this solemn warning of the future punishment of the ungodly. It was that we might not die, but turn and live.

Believe it, then, these words of the Son of God are true. They are spoken in love. They are spoken for your sake. Will you regard them? What if annihilation were the doom of the finally impenitent. Is there a soul that would desire it? You might accept this as a relief from suffering, but would you choose it as an alternative for bliss everlasting, when this lies freely before you in the Gospel? But you have not even this wretched choice. You cannot annihilate yourself: God will not annihilate you. Heaven and *hell* are set before you. Which do you choose? Soon you can no longer choose—but according to your decision here, will be welcomed there with the righteous into life eternal, or must go away into everlasting punishment.

LECTURE IX.

The Paternal Character of God a Pledge that He will punish Sin.

Rom. xi : 22. *Behold therefore the goodness and severity of God.*

The Biblical representation of God combines the qualities of Goodness and Severity as essential to his moral perfection. These qualities exist in the mind of God not in contrast but in harmony. They are not set off against each other as independent attributes naturally at variance, and each liable to be called out in its own way as occasion may arise, but they are both manifestations or expressons of the same character; and a character which was not capable of both expressions where moral subjects or actions are concerned, could not be complete. The "goodness" spoken of in the text is not the moral rectitude of God as a Being, but his good-will as a Sovereign, the benignity of his administration over this world. And his "severity" is not an abstract principle of justice, but a magisterial strictness against wrong-doing, which appears in the same administration. These two lines of action proceed from one and the same character. Several of the older English versions of the Bible—the Genevan of 1557, Cranmer's of 1539, and Tyndale's of 1534—here read "the *kindness* and *rigorousness* of God." The goodness of God is his gentleness or kindness seen in the dispensation of favors toward men; the severity of God is seen in the decisive expressions of his Providence against evil-doers. Either class of providential dispensations, taken alone, would make a partial, one-sided representation of the character of God. The *Goodness and Severity* of God, is the combined expression of his character which the apostle summons us to behold in the review of his Providence.

When our hearts bound with joy at the declaration that "God is love,"* we need to be reminded also that we should serve him acceptably, with reverence and godly fear,—for "our God is a consuming fire."†

The history of Theology exhibits the vibrations of the human mind between extreme views of the character of God. The sternest Calvinism and the loosest Liberalism find their types as far back at least as the fourth century;—Augustine dwelling upon the severer aspects of the divine character, and Pelagius seeing only its milder tones; the one contemplating all events from the point of absolute Predestination, the other from the point of absolute Free Will; the one viewing in Adam's sin the fall of mankind as a *totality* —from which only an elect portion could be redeemed, through the righteousness of Christ imputed to them by transfer;—the other regarding human nature as in a process of development which Christ assists " by the promulgation of a higher moral law, by present-

* I John iv : 8. † Hebrews xii 29.

ing new motives to virtue, and by giving an example of perfect morality, and an expression of the highest love for mankind." Each of these systems represented an extreme view. From one a severe logic would deduce fatalism; from the other rationalism; the one made God too exclusively a being of magisterial decrees; the other too exclusively a being of sentimental kindness; yet both combined the elements of important truths.

The Bible presents both paternal kindness and judicial rigor, in its representations of the character of God; but it presents these in combination, not in contrast. No single photograph can give a perfect likeness, for there are slight diversities between the two sides of every face; and not every feature can be brought exactly into focus upon the same plate, and therefore some part of the face is magnified out of proportion. When both sides of the face are taken at angles properly adjusted, and the two pictures are side by side in the stereoscope, then the *one* face stands out in the equalized proportions of nature. But if you look with one eye, through only one glass of the stereoscope, you see two pictures, or the confused outline of two. You must look with both eyes, through both lenses, upon both pictures at the same time, to see both combined into one distinct and well-proportioned representation. Now the Bible exhibits the character of God after the manner of the stereoscope. As I have before said, it nowhere sketches upon a single page a portrait of the divine character as complete; but it gives many views of God—each a transcript of some phase of his character, and each perhaps making prominent some one attribute. In this way his character is made to appear more real and life-like than if presented for contemplation in one elaborate picture. But we must be careful not to magnify a single feature or a group of features, this side or that, out of its proportion, and hold this up as if it were God. Just this is the mistake of the extremes of theology upon the governmental and the sentimental sides;—the one defining the character of God with too much of legal rigidity, the other with too lax a sentimentality. Now the Scriptures combine the essence of these two extreme theologies into one; not attempting to harmonize them as if they were at variance, but taking both the legal or judicial and the emotional aspects of the same divine character. Thus Paul catches the aspect of Goodness and the aspect of Severity, and then puts these together, side by side, under the lenses of the divine word, and says, —"Behold the goodness and severity of God;" and as you look, you see but one God in whom both these characteristics are blended. You cannot separate them, and retain a picture of God as He is;—the two attributes or manifestations are linked together by the copulative —*goodness and severity*—and God is the subject to whom these united attributes belong.

Such a presentation of the character of God —combining these two particular attributes,— is quite frequent in the Scriptures. When Jehovah revealed himself to the children of Israel in giving the law at Sinai, he said, "I the Lord thy God am a jealous God, visiting the iniquity of the fathers upon the children unto the third and fourth generation of them that hate me; and shewing mercy unto thousands of them that love me, and keep my commandments."* Again, when in answer to the petition of Moses that the Lord would show him his glory, Jehovah passed before him, he proclaimed himself "the Lord, the Lord God, merciful and gracious, long-suffering and abundant in goodness and truth, keeping mercy for thousands, forgiving iniquity and transgression and sin, and that will by no means clear the guilty; visiting the in iquity of the fathers upon the children, and upon the children's children unto the third and fourth generation."† The Psalms continually present these attributes in combination. "The Lord is gracious and full of compassion; slow to anger and of great mercy. The Lord is good to all: and his tender mercies are over all his works. The Lord is righteous in all his ways, and holy in all his works. The Lord preserveth all them that love him; but all the

* Exodus xx: 5, 6.   † Exodus xxxiv: 6, 7.

wicked will he destroy. The Lord openeth the eyes of the blind: the Lord raiseth them that are bowed down; the Lord loveth the righteous; the Lord preserveth the strangers; he relieveth the fatherless and widow; but the way of the wicked he turneth upside down."*

The New Testament, though peculiarly a revelation of mercy, combines these elements of goodness and severity in its delineations of the character of God. "God so loved the world, that he gave his only begotten Son, that whosoever believeth in him should not perish but have everlasting life. ... He that believeth on the Son hath everlasting life; and he that believeth not the Son shall not see life; but the wrath of God abideth upon him."† Love and wrath, compassion and mercy toward man as a fallen creature, righteous indignation toward the evil-doer and his works, Goodness and Severity—these are the ever-blending attributes of the one living and true God. Let us sum up here in one

* Psalm cxlv: 8, 9, 17, 20. Psalm cxlvi: 7—9.   † John iii: 16, 36

view the evidences of this combination which have been presented in previous lectures.

I. *We read these attributes on the face of nature.* The Alpine valley smiling with orchards and vineyards, watered with sunny brooks and fanned with mountain breezes; the overhanging cliffs girdled with storms, shaking down rocks and avalanches, and pouring torrents into the vale; these both are symbols of the divine author of creation, in his diverse aspects toward the moral world. The summer breeze that brings fragrance and health upon its wings, and fills the sails of commerce for an even sea; and the sudden gust that dashes the leviathan steamer like a potter's vessel, breaking her paddles and cracking her ribs, that lays low towers and steeples, unroofs palaces and buries human life beneath their ruins, that sweeps as a tornado across the prairies and scatters desolation and mourning in its track, making cities a heap and fruitful fields a wilderness, these both alike come from him "who maketh the clouds his chariot, and walketh upon the wings of the wind." Every where do we behold goodness and severity written upon the face of nature. You may seal up the Bible and blot out every record of God's character which the Bible has given to men; you may take the theology of Augustine and Turretin, of Calvin and Edwards, and of all believers in the moral government and the punitive justice of Jehovah, and bind it to a mill-stone and sink it in the depths of the sea; and you still read blazoned in great capitals over the earth and sky, The Goodness and Severity of God! The breeze whispers of his goodness and the storm howls with his severity; the sunbeam pencils his love, the volcano flames forth his consuming fire; the rainbow paints his mercy reaching like Jacob's ladder from earth to heaven, and the lightning flashes like the vengeance that licked up Sodom and Gomorrah.

No theology of nature has been able to divest itself of the sterner aspects of the divinity. We have seen that the old mythologies invented different classes of gods to represent phenomena in nature which seemed to them incongruous; peace and war, love and hate, light and darkness, health and sickness, good and evil, were severally represented by conflicting powers in the supernatural world. Or it was attempted by the theory of two opposing principles or forces in the universe to account for facts which could not be reconciled. But the *facts* remained; be there one God or many gods, be there a supreme being controlling all things or two opposite principles or incarnations of good and evil in perpetual conflict; still goodness and severity were there to be accounted for in any theology of nature.

If we introduce the scientific fiction of natural laws acting as causal or determinative *powers*, we only remove the difficulty one step further back. For a true science teaches that natural laws are only observed modes of uniformity in the operations of nature, and not original causes or powers; and we still demand, Who made laws or physical causes that produce storm and earthquake and pestilence and lightning and flood, and the long catalogue of natural evils? Does it at all relieve the difficulty or abate the severity of evil to say that Nature and not God produces it? What is nature? And whence this fatal power of mischief? Is it fixed by inevitable fate? Is it the whim and whirl of chance? You still have the goodness and severity, whether you oppose these on the battle-field of nature, or harmonize them in the attributes of God. And if mere blind Nature, or dumb physical law is armed with such fearful power of causality, and can wreak such mischief and wo at random, it is time there was a God to look after things—for such severity had better be coupled with intelligence to guide it and sympathy to modify it, than left to unintelligent and unfeeling nature!

2. *The goodness and severity of God appear in the providential history of mankind.* Without arguing the universality and particularity of divine Providence with respect to human affairs, I may confidently look for illustration of these two phases of the divine character to any individual life, and to those

salient points of general history upon which the Bible touches in the course of ages. Does not your own experience and observation in life illustrate both the Goodness and the Severity of God? If you acknowledge God's Providence at all, you must trace his hand in both pleasurable and afflictive experiences. Whose life has been so troubled that he has known nothing of mercy; has no record of kindnesses received from God? Or whose life has been so unruffled that he has had no taste of disappointment and sorrow? Or who will presume to argue from past mercies a future immunity from the ills of life? Does not each personal human history interblend the goodness and severity of God?

If we take the broad track of human history, we find this marked alike by the monuments of God's fraternal beneficence and of his judicial severity. The preservation of the human race, with an unwearying, unfailing supply for all its increase; the return of the seasons with the kindly fruits of the earth; the development of resources within the

15*

earth, stored there to meet the waste upon its surface; the application of science and invention to the facts and properties of nature, to supply an increasing population with reduced manual labor; the rain and sunshine, "filling our hearts with food and gladness;" these and unnumbered acts of bounty, bespeak the beneficence of God. But when we look upon another phase of the world, and see its early inhabitants swept away by the flood, and fire from heaven consuming Sodom and Gomorrah; when we see Pharaoh and his host swallowed up in the Red Sea, and a generation of Israelites wasted in the desert; when we see the idolatrous inhabitants of Canaan exterminated, and Israel falling into rebellion, scourged, scattered, peeled; when we follow the course of fulfilled prophecy, and find it like the track of a tornado over the mightiest cities and empires of antiquity, leaving Assyria, Babylon, Egypt, Tyre, Philistia, Edom, Greece, Rome, and even the land of promise ruined and forsaken; while we still behold the goodness of God lavished in the gifts of nature to these favored climes, we behold also his severity in stroke upon stroke of retribution for the iniquities of men. Goodness AND Severity is the lesson of human life, whether written in the smaller lines of individual experience, or the broader characters of national history.

3. *The blending of these characteristics is seen also in the peculiar dispensations of that system of Redemption recorded in the Scriptures.* It is this in particular that gives the apostle the illustration of the text. First, the *choosing* of Israel as the special depositary of divine revelation, and all the favor that attended them as the elect people—" the adoption, the glory, the covenants, the giving of the law, the divine service of the temple, and the promises"—then the *cutting off* of this same loved and chosen people because of unbelief; and the introducing into their place of favor and exaltation, of the Gentiles whom they had despised as outcasts and aliens;— this was an exhibition at once of the riches of divine mercy and the rigor of divine justice,

that might well make Paul—himself an Israelite of the seed of Abraham, and yet the apostle to the Gentiles—exclaim, "Behold therefore the goodness and severity of God: on them which fell severity; but toward thee, goodness, if thou continue in his goodness—otherwise thou also shalt be cut off." In the pathetic lamentations of the prophets over the doom of Israel, blending with their denunciations of the coming woe; in the tears of the Son of God mingling with his predictions of the destruction of Jerusalem—we see the goodness and severity of God mingling like the rainbow and the thunder in one cloud; even while the sun lights up the falling drops with sevenfold beauty, the lightning may dart its angry fire and smite to slay.

This union of Goodness and Severity in the divine character, which we trace alike in the administration of nature, of providence, and of grace, *is essential to the completeness of that character, and meets the requirements of our own moral nature in the Moral Governor of the universe.* As I have said, these characteristics are not opposites to be reconciled with each other—they are essentials, growing out of the same root in the pure and holy love of God. If it were said of a father,—he is all mildness and softness, never noticing anything amiss in his children, never reproving, punishing, or restraining them,—we should say that he was unequal to his duty, and that children were unfortunate in having such a father. If on the other hand it should be said of a father, that he was always stern and exacting, always governing by law and never by love, keeping his children at a distance, in almost servile subjection, we should pity the children of such a father, and deem him unworthy of his trust. But when we see kindness and rigorousness blended in the parental administration, we look for a well-ordered and happy.home. The apostle seizes upon this thought when contemplating the disciplinary measures which God employs with his people. ". Whom the Lord loveth he chasteneth, and scourgeth every son whom he receiveth."* "Severity" is strictly *a cutting short*—as by a precipice. In our own colloquial phrase, it denotes being "up and down" upon questions of right and principle. And surely a wise and gracious Father will have a will that is *up and down* upon questions of right and wrong.

The magistrate who administers only a code of terror and blood, and the magistrate who winks at the breach of law and is indifferent to crimes, are both disqualified for the place of authority. The harmonious blending of goodness and severity—the spirit of love and good-will breathing through the enactment—the rigorousness of authority against disobedience—these make the perfection of government.

> His spirit, when most severe, is oft most kind.
> As all authority in earth depends
> On Love and Fear, their several powers he blends,
> Copying with awe the one paternal mind.

If this be so under mere human government, how much more is it true under the

* Heb. xii : 6.

LOVE AND PENALTY. 351

moral government of God. The Governor of the universe must be "up and down" in his prohibition of wrong, "up and down" in his condemnation of the wrong-doer, "up and down" in the penalty that guards the sanctity of the law. His severity toward evil certifies the goodness of his character. Wordsworth has finely expressed this thought in one of his sonnets upon the appropriate penalty of laws fundamental to human society.

> What is a State ? The wise behold in her
> A creature born of time, that keeps one eye
> Fixed on the statutes of Eternity,
> To which her judgments reverently defer.
> Speaking through Law's dispassionate voice, the State
> Endues her conscience with external life
> And being, to preclude or quell the strife
> Of individual will, to elevate
> The groveling mind, the erring to recall,
> And *fortify the moral sense of all.*

And so, in a much loftier sense, in that sublime archetype of all government—the moral government of God—the statutes of Eternity speaking to the consciences of men through the dispassionate voice of Law, preclude or quell that strife of individual wills which would make the universe a chaos or a pandemonium, elevate the mind from groveling earthliness to its moral duties and its spiritual relationships, recall the erring by the admonition of penalty, and by the infliction of penalty upon the incorrigible, fortify the moral sense of the intelligent creation in holy obedience to the Right. In the severity of God we see "how awful goodness is."

That which calls forth the severity of God upon the wicked, is that very moral purity and benevolence which cause him to be characterized as Love. And it will be "a fearful thing" for incorrigible transgressors "to fall into the hands of the living God," not merely because of his justice, nor yet because of his power;—but because of the infinite purity of his character—because of his unchangeable love of holiness. This hatred of iniquity can know no change or abatement. His love forbids that it should ever come to an end. Mere anger might subside. The vindication of personal honor might at length be satisfied. But love cannot die—love will not change ; and the love of God for holiness, and his goodness toward his creatures demand the emphatic severity of his displeasure against sin. God will be a consuming fire to the wicked, because of the instinctive, the intense, the unconquerable repulsion between holiness and sin, between a mind that loves purity and goodness, and a mind that loves iniquity. The doctrine of the future punishment of the wicked is therefore philosophically a credible doctrine. So far from being contradicted by the known character of God, it is a direct inference from his benevolence and integrity as a moral Governor.

In summing up the argument of these lectures, I remark—

1. *Christians should study the great principles of God's government as a means of spiritual strength.* The inward tone of our piety is strengthened by grasping vigorously and earnestly these foundation truths of love and penalty, goodness and severity. Strong views of sin, strong views of law, lead to strong

love for Christ and strong devotion to the redemptive scheme as revealed in the Gospel. There is no love for Christ, for truth, for goodness, there is no confiding and adoring love for God as a Father, like that which flows from a heart that feels and owns its desert of all the condemnation that the Bible threatens against sin, yet rejoices in all the grace the Gospel brings to it in the cross.

Strength for philanthropic endeavor is gained by intelligently grasping these grand principles of God's government. That is no sickly sentimentalism upon the one hand, and no scorning, denunciatory self-righteousness upon the other, which represents the philanthropy of the gospel. That philanthropy takes a deeper tone of sympathy and tenderness from the thought that men are dead in trespasses and sins, lying under condemnation for their guilt; and it takes also a loftier hope and a holier earnestness from the thought that " the Son of Man came to seek and to save that which was lost." Guilt is a word of deeper significance than misery: sin is sadder far than sorrow; and therefore the gospel that shows man under the guilt and ruin of sin, stirs the heart of the believer to strongest compassion, and the most earnest endeavor for the perishing. This view of mankind as guilty, condemned, and liable to eternal punishment for their sins—the view presented by Paul in the first chapter of Romans—is the only view that can give strength, permanence, and vitality to the missionary enterprise. The doctrine of eternal punishment ministers to the spiritual strength and the benevolent activity of all who truly receive it.

2. *Christians should cherish a compassionate tenderness for the souls of their fellow-men.* There is undoubtedly in the minds of many a shrinking from the whole truth of the Bible concerning the state and prospects of the ungodly. *They* perceive this in the comparative indifference of many Christians to *their* position as sinners, and hence they begin to doubt whether the declarations of the Bible on this subject are true, and whether Chris-

tians really believe them. But these momentous truths are to be held not logically nor sentimentally alone, but with a compassionate tenderness toward all who are yet living in their sins—a tenderness inspired by the consciousness of having escaped the same impending doom, through the grace which can deliver them also. Hence a right view of future punishment does not make one gloomy and desponding touching the condition of his fellow-men; but rather like the physician in a critical but not hopeless case—watchful, earnest, sympathetic, devoted to save. He who views this doctrine from the true standpoint in the love of God, will be moved thereby to the intensest love for man. He who would preach this doctrine as Christ declared it must be in fullest sympathy with Christ as he wept over Jerusalem.

3. *The fact that the eternal punishment of the wicked is declared with such solemnity and pathos by Christ himself, should lead all men at once to forsake their sins and to seek the mercy of God through the Redeemer.*

That God is in earnest in the warnings of his word, who can doubt that reads the accusations of his own conscience, the lessons of retribution in history, or the lesson of redemption in the tears and agony and blood of Gethsemane and Calvary? That Christ is in earnest in calling sinners to repentance that they may not perish forever, who can doubt, that studies his life of patient and watchful love and his death of voluntary sacrifice? And shall not men be in earnest to save that for which the Divine Nature—Creator, Redeemer, Lord—is stirred with such earnestness of warning and entreaty? Who can be indifferent to the thought of an eternal hell deserved by his sins? Who can be unmoved at the sight of the cross of Christ uplifted for his redemption? All the great things of earth and time are as nothing compared with the greatness of our peril by sin, the greatness of our redemption by Christ. How then shall we escape if we neglect so great salvation? The voice of the Infinite Father hath declared:

HE THAT BELIEVETH ON THE SON HATH EVERLASTING LIFE; AND HE THAT BELIEVETH NOT THE SON, SHALL NOT SEE LIFE; BUT THE WRATH OF GOD ABIDETH ON HIM.

FINIS.

Books Published by Sheldon & Co.

FORTY YEARS' EXPERIENCE IN SUNDAY-SCHOOLS.

BY STEPHEN H. TYNG, D.D.,

Rector of St. George's Church, New York.

1 neat 16mo vol., price 60 cents.

From the Boston Gazette.

"As a matter of course, the volume is in a measure autobiographical, which would alone secure general attention to it."

From the Southern Churchman.

"No one is entitled to speak about Sunday-schools with more authority than Dr. Tyng, and no one can read this volume without obtaining most valuable hints for the management of a Sunday-school."

From the Boston Courier.

"This little work of a distinguished divine will doubtless prove of great service to superintendents and teachers of Sunday-schools."

From the Troy Times.

"In a literary point of view, they are marked by all the excellencies for which the reverend author is noted; while the amount of real, useful knowledge they convey in a brief and practical form, upon a subject the importance of which is little understood, is really surprising."

From the N. Y. Intelligencer.

"Few pastors have been favored with so large a measure of experience and success in the work of Sabbath-school instruction as the venerable pastor of St. George's Church. As the present volume contains the results of the author's long experience, it will be a welcome addition to our Sabbath-school literature."

From the N. Y. Independent.

"Every Sabbath-school teacher should read it; every pastor might profit by it."

From the N. Y. Observer.

"This will be a very welcome volume to Sunday-school teachers, and to all who are interested in Sunday-schools. It embodies the experience and the counsels of one who, by his deep interest in the cause, and by a personal devotion to the work, even in its details, and by a success which has been rarely if ever equaled, is qualified to speak with great profit upon the important subject. We have often made mention of the school at St. George's church, as perhaps the largest in the country, and as exhibiting results, not only in the chief end of Sabbath-school instruction, but in the great work of Christian benevolence and Christian activity, which are delightful to contemplate. In these pages the author imparts, in a measure, the secret of his success. We are sure that the volume has a great mission to accomplish for good."

Books Published by Sheldon & Co.

ABBOTT'S AMERICAN HISTORY.

A Series of American Histories for Youth, by JACOB ABBOTT, in 12 volumes. Price 75 cents each. Each volume complete in itself.

Illustrated by numerous maps and engravings, from original designs, by Darley, Chapin, Perkins, Stephens, Herrick, Parsons, Mullin, and others.

1. Aboriginal America.
2. Discovery of America.
3. The Northern Colonies.
4. The Southern Colonies.
5. Revolt of the Colonies.
6. Boston in Seventy-Five.
7. New York in Seventy-Six.
8. The Carolinas in Seventy-Nine.
9. Campaign in the Jerseys.
10. Expedition of Burgoyne.
11. Surrender of Cornwallis.
12. The Federal Constitution.

In press, to be issued at an early day.

ABORIGINAL AMERICA is now ready.

The Publishers, in presenting this Series of popular American Histories for Youth, believe that they are supplying a want long felt in our country, and one which no author living is so well able to fill as JACOB ABBOTT, the popular author of so many juvenile books. Mr. ABBOTT has given more than usual care in the preparation of this Series, and they will be illustrated in the best manner, it being the intention of the Publishers to make them as attractive as they will be useful and entertaining.

THE SUNNY SIDE SERIES.

By Mrs. E. STUART PHELPS and CARA BELMONT.

Peep at No. 5,
Last Leaf from Sunny Side,
Tell Tale,
City Side.

4 vols. 18mo, uniform style. Price of each 50 cents.

Books Published by Sheldon & Co.

WAY MARKS
TO APOSTOLIC BAPTISM;

Or, Historical Testimonies, Demonstrating the Original Form of the Rite, as Ordained by our Lord Jesus Christ, and Administered by His Holy Apostles.

1 vol. 18mo. Price 35 cents.

From GEO. W. EATON, D.D., *President of Madison University.*

"It is a happy conception, admirably and thoroughly worked out, within a compass which renders the whole historical argument relating to 'Apostolic Baptism' acceptable to the general reader."

From WM. CAREY CRANE, D.D., *President of Mt. Lebanon (La.) University.*

"I think it happily adapted to that large class of inquirers in our congregations who have neither the learning nor the time for the careful perusal and study of more elaborate works. For a work of so small a compass it appears to embrace a vast amount of matter, and is arranged with due pecision and order."

From A. C. KENDRICK, D.D., *Professor in Rochester University.*

"Its circulation among the Churches must do good; it will show Baptists the strength of their position, and have a strong tendency to convince doubters. It is a good little book, and the better for being small."

From RICHARD FULLER, D.D., *of Baltimore.*

"As a brief compendium of argument which might fill a large treatise it may be employed most effectually. The arrangement seems to be very judicious, and the author has shown very rare talents. He is concise, and his arguments have been carefully authenticated."

From D. R. CAMPBELL, D.D., *President of Georgetown (Ky.) College.*

"I deem it a perfect Thesaurus of testimony on the subject of which it treats. It will be invaluable in the hands of the people and the great body of our ministers."

From J. B. JETER, D.D., *of Richmond, Va.*

"It is worthy of general circulation, and especially of a place in the library of every Baptist minister who has not access to the numerous and rare works from which its contents are selected."

From JAMES P. BOYCE, D.D., *President of Greenville (S. C.) Seminary.*

"The 'Way Marks' has many excellencies, and is well worthy of general circulation. It seems to have been carefully prepared, and that' too, by one who seeks original sources of information. It might have been much enlarged, but I can scarcely see how the author could have used to greater advantage the space he has taken up."

Books Published by Sheldon & Co.

THE BAPTIST CHURCH DIRECTORY.
A Guide to the Doctrines, Discipline, Officers, Ordinances, and Customs of Baptist Churches. By EDWARD T. HISCOX, D. D Price, red edges, 60 cents; plain, 50 cents.

"It will prove, in my judgment, an invaluable guide to our church members."—*Dr. Jeter, of Richmond.*

LIFE OF SPENCER H. CONE, D. D. With
a fine Steel Plate Portrait. 1 vol. 12mo. Price $1 25.

"A complete, accurate, and in every way reliable memoir of our lamented brother."—*New York Chronicle.*

GRACE TRUMAN; or, Love and Principle.
By SALLIE ROCHESTER FORD. With Steel Portrait of the Authoress. 1 vol. 12mo. Price $1.

PRINCIPLES AND PRACTICES OF BAPTISTS.
By FRANCIS WAYLAND, D. D. 1 vol. 12mo. Price, $1.

THE BAPTIST DENOMINATION. By
Rev. D. C. HAYNES. With an Introduction by Rev. JOHN DOWLING, D. D. 1 vol. 12mo. Price $1.

THE BAPTIST LIBRARY. A Republication
of Standard Baptist Works. Edited by Rev. Messrs G. G. SOMERS, W. R. WILLIAMS, and L. L. HILL. 1 vol. royal octavo. Sheep. $3 50.

BENEDICT'S HISTORY OF THE BAPTISTS.
A General History of the Baptist Denomination in America, and other parts of the World. By DAVID BENEDICT. With a Steel Portrait of Roger Williams. 1 vol. royal octavo. Sheep. Price $3 50.

COMPENDIUM OF THE FAITH OF THE
BAPTISTS. Paper. Price, per dozen, 50 cents.

Books Published by Sheldon & Co.

SUMMER PICTURES FROM COPENHAGEN TO VENICE. By Rev. HENRY M. FIELD. 1 vol. 12mo. Price, $1.

"Mr. Field's Pictures have been drawn with a graphic pen, and the book, we doubt not, will be everywhere wanted."—*Christian Intelligencer.*

"A delightful book—the work of an enlightened, liberal-minded man, who travels to some purpose for others as well as for himself. * * * The style is very clear and pointed, and is devoid of all superfluous words."—*Boston Traveller.*

THE LOSING AND TAKING OF MANSOUL; or, Lectures on the Holy War. By Rev A. S. PATTON, A.M. 1 vol. 12mo. Illustrated with Eight spirited Engravings. Price $1.

"He writes well and forcibly."—*Philadelphia Ledger.*

"The eminent author of this work has compressed into a brief space a comprehensive review of the evils which, without religious influences, everywhere abound in society, and the effective means with which to correct them. It is the result of a life-time of deep thought and close observation."—*Dubuque Times.*

THE "PRECIOUS STONES OF THE HEAVENLY FOUNDATIONS." By AUGUSTA BROWN GARRET. 1 vol. 18mo. Price $1.

"A book of great beauty, and full of attractive discourse on heavenly and divine things."—*New York Observer.*

"The articles are brief, and include many choice specimens of prose and poetry. It is especially adapted to lay on the center-table, or elsewhere, for the casual reader."—*Congregationalist.*

"The book is a suggestive one, and needs but a slight examination to become a favorite with the religious portion of the community."—*Boston Post.*

MEMOIR OF REV. DAVID T. STODDARD By Rev. J. P. THOMPSON, D. D. 1 vol. 12mo. Price $1.

"A biography of serene beauty and abiding value."—*New Englander.*

"All Sabbath School libraries and all students should especially make sure of the possession of this volume."—*Congregationalist.*

"The entire volume proffers numerous claims to an extended circulation."—*North American.*

Books Published by Sheldon & Co.

BLIND BARTIMEUS; Or, The Story of a
Sightless Sinner and his Great Physician. By Rev. WILLIAM J. HOGE, Professor in the Union Theological Seminary, Prince Edwards, Va. 1 vol. large 18mo. 257 pages. 75 cents.

"A most excellent book, full of sound instruction and the very spirit of the Gospel."—*Boston Recorder.*
"We wish it could be placed, this winter, in the hands of thousands of 'sightless sinners.'"—*Cincinnati Christian Herald.*
"Brief in compass, clear in arrangement, and singularly animated, direct, forcible, and pungent in style, not rarely reminding one of the fervor of Richard Baxter, while marked throughout by a classic elegance of diction, to which he made no pretension."—*Cor. N. C. Presbyterian.*

DAILY THOUGHTS FOR A CHILD. By
Mrs. THOMAS GELDART, author of "Truth is Every Thing," "Emilie the Peacemaker," etc., etc. 1 vol. 18mo. 50 cents.

"In exquisite simplicity of style, beauty of illustration, and religious power, this book has few superiors in juvenile literature."—*Boston Era.*
"Meditations for morning and evening for a month, adapted to the capacity and aspirations of a youthful heart. Many of them are very sweet and affecting compositions."
"A charming little work, which is sure to be a favorite with the young."—*English Papers.*

TRUTH IS EVERY THING. By Mrs.
THOMAS GELDART. 1 vol. 18mo. Price 50 cents.

"The interest of the volume is genuine. There is nothing false or spurious about it. It is true to nature; it is true to the heart."
"This is a charming little book for the young; the matter is very interesting, not overdrawn, while its tenor is to win over youth to the practice and love of truth."
"This is a charming tale, attractive from the simplicity and beauty of feeling which pervades it—most useful because it steps not beyond the comprehension of youth."—*English Press.*

THE LIVING EPISTLE; or, The Moral
Power of a Religious Life. By Rev. CORNELIUS TYREE, of Powhatan, Va. With an Introduction by Rev. Dr. FULLER, of Baltimore. 1 vol. 18mo. Price 60 cents.

"It is adapted to the wants of the times, and, we trust, will be extensively read."—*Southern Baptist Missionary Magazine.*
"A book full of good counsels, important lessons, elevating the idea of the Christian life, and encouraging the reader to holy living and action."—*New York Observer.*

Books Published by Sheldon & Co.

THE CHRISTIAN GRACES. By Rev. J. P. Thompson, D.D., of the Broadway Tabernacle. 1 vol 18mo. Price 75 cents.

"The book is well fitted to do good to all everywhere; and we hope it will be widely read, and made greatly useful."—*New York Observer.*

"Dr. Thompson has a happy talent for the familiar exposition of Scripture, and the practical application of its doctrines."—*Boston Recorder.*

"They are earnest and affectionate exhortations, intended to help in the formation of Christian character, and the cultivation of the Christian graces."—*Boston Advertiser.*

THE BIBLE IN THE LEVANT; or, The Life and Letters of Rev. Chester N. Righter. By Rev. S. Irenæus Prime, D.D. Illustrated with a Steel Portrait of Mr. Righter. 1 vol. 18mo. 336 pages. Price 75 cents.

"The results of his efforts are narrated by Mr. Prime in a style clear and interesting, which renders this volume not only readable, but exceedingly instructive. We can commend the work with entire confidence that it will be productive of good results."—*Boston Post.*

"It is really beautiful in its delineation of a frank, whole-souled man, who always pressed straight forward in the fear of God, without any fear of man."—*Hartford Courant.*

"Mr. Righter's visit to the Copts, in Egypt, and description of that interesting people, will be read with peculiar interest. The account of his travels is taken principally from his letters, and displays, unconsciously, his bold, fearless, unwavering devotion to the right. His biographer was his traveling companion in his first tour abroad, and enjoyed peculiar advantages for thoroughly comprehending his character."—*Boston Journal*

GLIMPSES OF JESUS, EXALTED IN THE AFFECTIONS OF HIS PEOPLE. By Rev. W. P Balfern. 1 vol. 18mo. Price 60 cents.

"This book is redolent with the sweet savor of Him whose name is like precious ointment poured forth."—*Evangelical Repository.*

"Few works of this class are to be named with it, and as a Sabbath School volume it stands, we should think, almost without a rival."—*Boston Daily Traveller.*

"This is a sweet little book. Many a halting pilgrim will be quickened, many awakened ones will be led to Jesus, and many stricken souls will be revived and comforted by a perusal of its pages, beaming with a Saviour's love."—*Presbyterian Banner and Advocate.*

"It presents the example of Christ under the various circumstances and vicissitudes of his brief earthly history, for the imitation and encouragement of his followers."—*American Presbyterian and Genesee Evangelist.*

Books Published by Sheldon & Co.

THE CHINA MISSION; embracing a History of the various Missions of all Denominations among the Chinese, with Biographical Sketches of deceased Missionaries. By WILLIAM DEAN, D.D., twenty years a Missionary to China. 1 vol. 12mo. Price, $1.

"The author has looked with the eye of a practical teacher upon the land and the people he was to conquer, and he has given us what we feel is a true and living portraiture of the habits, customs, and traditions of the nation. * * * Aside from its religious aspect, this work has an attractiveness and novelty that is rarely surpassed by any publication."—*Albany Statesman*.

"Enjoying advantages of information possessed by few others in like degree, he has grouped together a statement of facts remarkable for its conciseness, clearness, and graphic method of presentation. His book is as interesting as that of M. Huc, and perhaps much more entirely veracious. It will add greatly to our knowledge of the remarkable nation of which it treats."—*Troy Times*.

SUNDAY MORNING THOUGHTS. By Mrs. THOMAS GELDART, author of "Emilie the Peacemaker" etc. 1 vol. 16mo. Price, 50 cents.

SUNDAY EVENING THOUGHTS. By Mrs THOMAS GELDART, author of "Truth is Everything," etc. 1 vol. 16mo. Price, 50 cents.

EMILIE THE PEACEMAKER. By Mrs. THOMAS GELDART. 1 vol. 16mo. Price, 50 cents.

"This beautiful story excels almost all the moral and religious tales we know. The best things of Mrs. Sherwood and Mrs. Hofland are in many respects inferior to it; and Miss Edgeworth seldom wrote more vigorously and charmingly; while, in purity of sentiment and exquisite illustration of the truth it embodies, it is richer far than are the works of the writers we have named. Seldom has a great lesson been more touchingly taught, or piety of heart and life been rendered more attractive."—*Nonconformist*.

"We know not when we have read a tale so entirely to our mind as this. The lesson conveyed in the tale is one of heavenly wisdom, inculcating 'peace upon earth, and good-will towards men,' and the heart of every reader must be improved by it."—*Norfolk News*.

THE WORDS OF JESUS AND THE FAITHFUL PROMISER. By the Author of "The Morning and Night Watches." 1 vol. 18mo. Price 37 cents.

STODDARD'S SERIES OF ARITHMETICS,

AND STODDARD & HENKLE'S

ALGEBRAS,

Have become deservedly popular. They are now extensively used in the Public and Private Schools of the following cities:

DETROIT,	MICH.,	NASHVILLE,	TENN.,
ANN ARBOR,	"	ST. LOUIS,	MO.,
GRAND RAPIDS,	"	CHARLESTON,	S. C.,
ADRIAN,	"	TORONTO,	C. W.,
YPSILANTI,	"	HAMILTON,	C. W.,
CLEVELAND,	OHIO.	BALTIMORE,	MD.,
COLUMBUS,	"	ALBANY,	N. Y.,
CINCINNATI,	"	BROOKLYN,	"
LEXINGTON,	KY.,	ROCHESTER,	"
LOUISVILLE,	"	NEW YORK,	"

And a host of smaller cities and towns throughout the Union.

The authors (Profs. John F. Stoddard of New York, and W. D. Henkle of Ohio) are practical and accomplished teachers, and the popularity of their books is evinced by the annual sale, throughout the United States and the Canadas, of nearly

150,000 COPIES.

The Series consists of

The Juvenile Mental Arithmetic, for Primary Schools. Price 12 cents.

The American Intellectual Arithmetic, an extended work, designed for Common Schools, Seminaries, and Academies. Price 20 cents.

Stoddard's Practical Arithmetic, which embraces every variety of exercises appropriate to written Arithmetic. Price 40 cents.

RECOMMENDATIONS.

Stoddard's Philosophical Arithmetic, a higher work for Colleges and advanced Classes in Union Schools, Seminaries, and Academies. Price 60 cents.

Key to Stoddard's Intellectual and Practical Arithmetic, in one book. Price 50 cents.

Stoddard and Henkle's Elementary Algebra, for the use of Common Schools and Academies, by JOHN F. STODDARD, A.M., and PROFESSOR W. D. HENKLE, of Ohio South-Western Normal School. Price 75 cents.

Stoddard and Henkle's University Algebra, the most thorough work on Algebra ever published in this country, for High Schools, Academies, and Colleges. By JOHN F. STODDARD, A.M., and PROFESSOR W. D. HENKLE, of Ohio South-Western Normal School. Price $1 50.

The series, as a whole, by a truly progressive arrangement and classification of examples, including the various kinds and combinations in compound and complex ratios, or "Double Position," original methods of computing interest, discount, and percentage, in all their variations, together with a variety of Algebraic exercises, is carefully designed to conduct the learner from initiatory steps, by an easy and gradually progressive system, to the more advanced attainments in Mathematical Science.

The Elementary Algebra bears the relation to this science that Stoddard's Intellectual Arithmetic does to that of numbers. Systematic in its arrangement, concise and clear in its solutions and demonstrations, and abounding with exercises and practical questions of original combinations, it will be found a desirable addition to the text-books on this subject now before the public.

The University Algebra, containing an extensive collection of practical examples, is the most extensive treatise on the subject ever published in America. It is an encyclopedia of Algebraic Science, the authors having consulted, in its preparation, upwards of two hundred works of the best French, German, and English authors.

Every teacher should possess a copy of this work, for consultation and reference, whatever other works he may use.

RECOMMENDATIONS.

From W. H. Boies, Hennepin, Ill.
"Your series of Arithmetics I am better pleased with than any other I ever examined or used."

From J. J. Sadler, Sturgis U. School, St. Joseph Co., Mich.
"For the past six years I have used 'Stoddard's Series of Arithmetics' in the school-room, and after examination of other arithmetics, both mental and written, I find none so well suited for use in classes as Stoddard's, especially the Juvenile Mental and American Intellectual."

From John Gordon, Principal of United Grammar and Common Schools, Port Hope, C. W.
"We have adopted Stoddard's Arithmetics and like them very much, and our example is being followed by most of the District Schools in the county."

From Morris C. Sulphur, Prof. of Mathematics in College of New Jersey.
"Stoddard's University Algebra, for beauty and symmetry of arrangement, and clearness of demonstration, surpasses any that I have ever met. It is eminently fitted to give a comprehensive knowledge of the whole science of Algebra, and a thorough understanding of its principles. I trust that it will receive a patronage corresponding with its merit."

From Prof. J. S. Van Dyke.
"I concur in the above."

From E. D. B. Porter, Indiana Co., Penn.
"I have examined Stoddard & Henkle's Elementary Algebra carefully, and have found it, as I expected, the best work published on the subject of Elementary Algebra. The introductory sections form an excellent intellectual Algebra, which is a desideratum. * * * But I need not specify the particular points which I admire, as the work, in all its parts, is superior to any other with which I am acquainted."

From G. H. Hartupee, Prof. Math., Baldwin's University.
"I have examined some portions of Stoddard & Henkle's University Algebra, and am delighted with it. I think it the most thorough and comprehensive work on the subject with which I am acquainted. To him who would be master of this department of Mathematics, this book or its equivalent is essential. I have never before met with a text-book in Algebra so well adapted to make students thorough."

From D. B. Hagar, Jamaica Plain, Mass.
"I have had time to examine Stoddard & Henkle's University Algebra, and so much has it pleased me, that I am making use of it in my school-room. The problems it contains are admirable, and the *logical* character of the work strikes me as remarkably good."

From M. Judson Vincent, Erie, Mich.
"I have thoroughly examined Stoddard's University Algebra, and for the last two months tested its merits in the school-room. I know of no work on Algebra that is so eminently fitted for the uses of the school-room as this. It is very thorough, methodical, and concise in all its parts; and I have no hesitancy in saying it is the best work of the kind published in this country."

From Geo. A. Chase, Pres. Brookville College.
"I have no hesitation in saying that I am highly pleased with the University Algebra. I admire the arrangement of the work, the clearness of the demonstrations, and the evident aim of the authors to impart to the student the ability to understand and apply Algebraic principles. One of the best features of the Algebra, as a class book, is the great and variety of practical examples."

RECOMMENDATIONS.

"NEW YORK, July 18, 1853.
"After a careful examination of 'Stoddard's Practical Arithmetic,' I have no hesitation in pronouncing it a work of very superior merit. The brevity and clearness of its definitions and rules, its lucid analysis of every operation, and the great variety of its examples, comprising almost every possible combination of arithmetical principles, render it one of the best books to discipline the mind of the scholar, in mathematical reasoning, I have ever seen. HENRY KIDDLE."

"July 15, 1853.
"I entirely concur with Mr. Kiddle in his opinion of 'Stoddard's Practical Arithmetic.' H. FANNING."

"I also concur with Mr. Kiddle in his opinion of 'Stoddard's Practical Arithmetic.' DAVID PATTERSON, Prin. P. S. No. 3."

"I concur in the above. GEO. MOORE."

From Professor Drew, of the City of New York.
"To Colburn belongs the honor of introducing the system of Intellectual Arithmetic, and to Stoddard the honor of perfecting that system. If Colburn opened a new road to mathematical science, Stoddard has leveled that road, and strewn it with flowers."

From S. A. Terrel, Supt. Pub. Schools, Wayne Co., Pa.
"Stoddard's Arithmetical Series are now in general use in the schools of this county. They have stood the test for four years as the text-books on arithmetic in our schools, and are considered by our teachers superior to any others now before the public."

From E. A. Lawrence, Scranton, Pa.
"I have examined your Arithmetics, especially the Practical, with considerable care, and, I am free to say, with great satisfaction. I think you have *succeeded* in doing what you proposed—'to set forth correctly, concisely and clearly the principles of numbers.'"

From J. T. Briggs, B.A., Principal of Wayne Co. Normal School.
"Having used Prof. J. F. Stoddard's Arithmetical Series for several terms, I am prepared to say, they are works of superior merit, and would aid much in advancing the cause of education if they were introduced into all the schools of the State. The works are systematic and progressive in their arrangement, and thorough in their treatment of the science of numbers. The Intellectual Arithmetic I consider the 'ne plus ultra' of arithmetics."

From Geo. F. M'Farland, McAlisterville, Pa.
"We have now been using Prof. Stoddard's Juvenile, Mental, and Intellectual Arithmetics about two years, and have no hesitancy in pronouncing them the *best* works of the kind with which we are acquainted. They have fully met our expectations in every particular, answering the necessities of every class of students, including our dull, plodding Germans, who often form a considerable portion of our classes. The Practical is now used more than any other in the Academy, and gives entire satisfaction."

From Wm. Elliott, Jr., Prof. Math. C. High School, Baltimore, Md.
"Of the Mental Arithmetics I can speak *now* and *emphatically*, in terms of high commendation. I know of no book of the kind in the language *comparable* with it."

www.ingramcontent.com/pod-product-compliance
Lightning Source LLC
Chambersburg PA
CBHW020302240426
43673CB00039B/682